What people a

Rebalance: How Women Lead, Parent, Partner and Thrive

"Finally, a roadmap for working mothers and fathers seeking to balance meaningful careers, raise good children, give back to society and practice self-care in an ever-changing world. In *Rebalance,* Lisa, Monica, and Wendy beautifully articulate a paradigm for understanding what each of us want out of life when it comes to family, work, friendships and more – and how to adjust when those desires evolve over time."
Nancy Cordes, Chief White House Correspondent, CBS News

"For those striving to live more fully as parents, professionals and partners, *Rebalance* provides thoughtful tips, real-world examples, inspiring stories and wisdom to help gain perspective, change routines, and re-calibrate towards a more fulfilled (and less guilt-ridden) future. Thank you Lisa, Monica, and Wendy for this book!"
Elizabeth Maw, President, Presidio Graduate School

"The phrase 'work-life balance' is one of my biggest pet peeves: It suggests a 50/50 equilibrium that leads you inevitably to do each side poorly. In *Rebalance,* you'll instead learn about 'the edge of the wheel' – an incredibly useful tool to gauge and manage your ever-shifting priorities among work, community, family, and self. This inspiring, accessible, and informative book written by three pioneering women will give you the permission to pursue a life of meaning, the courage to take risks, and, yes, the license to THRIVE!"
Linda Rottenberg, Author, *Crazy Is a Compliment: The Power of Zigging When Everyone Else Zags,* CEO, Co-Founder, Endeavor

"When women are supported to bring their whole selves to work, family, friendship and community, they create magic and a better world. Rebalance covers the joys and challenges of living a full life of purpose with authenticity and vulnerability. This powerful book offers lessons on living a full life of purpose through personal stories and reflections from three women leaders to their sisters, their communities, and all those who will cherish this gem."

Maya Chorengel, Co-Managing Partner, The Rise Funds, TPG

"For leaders looking to amplify their impact, this is a 'must read' book. It offers authentic accounts alongside strategies and tactics for how to grow professionally and personally as you make your mark in the world."

Fiona M. Macaulay, Founder-CEO, WILD Network, Adjunct Professor, McDonough School of Business, Georgetown University

"Every executive with children strives for balance and to make it all work. Rebalance is a recipe for getting it done – excelling at work, being present for family, and carving out time for oneself."

Ellen Weinreb, Managing Director, Weinreb Group Sustainability Recruiting

"This book is coming at an important time as we emerge from cocoons after a pandemic, lifting the veil behind how working mothers combine it all and thrive. It is not easy to attain excellence in work, family and children let alone thrive during the process. Thank you to Wendy, Lisa and Monica for their authentic honest reflections so we can learn from the very relevant experiences of three working women road warriors."

Momina Aijazuddin, Global Head Microfinance, IFC

"In 2010, a group of ambitious, socially conscious women came together in DC. Their goal was to help each other balance a family-focused life with meaningful careers. Drawing on their stories of success and setbacks over a decade, the three authors share their 'aha' moments, their lessons learned and help us feel that anything is possible as long as we follow our 'true north.' I recommend it to any woman (or man) seeking to live life with purpose."
Stephanie J. Miller, Author, *Zero Waste Living: the 80/20 Way*, Former Director, IFC

"The great thinker Khalil Gibran said, 'Work is love made visible.' The stories and lessons of Rebalance are an inspirational guide for how to achieve a complete overlap of the personal and the professional, and for how to be reflective on the paths we pursue and those we intentionally leave behind."
Mona Mourshed, Founding Global CEO, Generation

"Rebalance holds true for our individual lives and serves as a mantra for how to change our economy as a whole — towards one where business serves society and not the reverse."
Saskia Thais Bruysten, Co-Founder & CEO, Yunus Social Business

RESETTING OUR FUTURE

Rebalance

How Women Lead, Parent,
Partner and Thrive

RESETTING OUR FUTURE

Rebalance

How Women Lead, Parent, Partner and Thrive

Monica Brand Engel

Lisa Neuberger Fernandez

Wendy Teleki

CHANGEMAKERS
BOOKS

Winchester, UK
Washington, USA

JOHN HUNT PUBLISHING

First published by Changemakers Books, 2022
Changemakers Books is an imprint of John Hunt Publishing Ltd., No. 3 East Street,
Alresford, Hampshire SO24 9EE, UK
office@jhpbooks.com
www.johnhuntpublishing.com
www.changemakers-books.com

For distributor details and how to order please visit the 'Ordering' section on our website.

Text copyright: Lisa Neuberger Fernandez, Monica Brand Engel, Wendy Teleki 2022

ISBN: 978 1 80341 042 5
978 1 80341 043 2 (ebook)
Library of Congress Control Number: 2021947482

A CIP catalogue record for this book is available from the British Library.

Design: Matthew Greenfield

UK: Printed and bound by CPI Group (UK) Ltd, Croydon, CR0 4YY
Printed in North America by CPI GPS partners

We operate a distinctive and ethical publishing philosophy in
all areas of our business, from our global network of authors to
production and worldwide distribution.

Contents

The *Resetting Our Future* Series

At this critical moment of history, with a pandemic raging, we have the rare opportunity for a Great Reset – to choose a different future. This series provides a platform for pragmatic thought leaders to share their vision for change based on their deep expertise. For communities and nations struggling to cope with the crisis, these books will provide a burst of hope and energy to help us take the first difficult steps towards a better future.

Tim Ward, publisher, Changemakers Books

What if Solving the Climate Crisis Is Simple?

Tom Bowman, President of Bowman Change, Inc., and writing-team lead for the U.S. ACE National Strategic Planning Framework

Zero Waste Living, the 80/20 Way

The Busy Person's Guide to a Lighter Footprint

Stephanie Miller, Founder of Zero Waste in DC, and former Director, IFC Climate Business Department

A Chicken Can't Lay a Duck Egg

How COVID-19 Can Solve the Climate Crisis

Graeme Maxton, former Secretary-General of the Club of Rome, and Bernice Maxton-Lee, former Director, Jane Goodall Institute

A Global Playbook for the Next Pandemic

Anne Kabagambe, former World Bank Executive Director

Power Switch

How We Can Reverse Extreme Inequality

Paul O'Brien, Executive Director, Amnesty International USA

Impact ED
*How Community College Entrepreneurship
Creates Equity and Prosperity*
Rebecca Corbin, President & CEO, National Association of
Community College Entrepreneurship, Andrew Gold and
Mary Beth Kerly, both business faculty,
Hillsborough Community College

Empowering Climate Action in the United States
Tom Bowman, President of Bowman Change, Inc. and Deb
Morrison, Learning Scientist, University of Washington

Learning from Tomorrow
*Using Strategic Foresight to Prepare for
the Next Big Disruption*
Bart Édes, former North American Representative,
Asian Development Bank

Cut Super Climate Pollutants, Now!
*The Ozone Treaty's Urgent Lessons for
Speeding Up Climate Action*
Alan Miller, former World Bank representative for global
climate negotiations, Durwood Zaelke, President and founder,
the Institute for Governance & Sustainable Development, and
Stephen O. Andersen, former Director of Strategic Climate
Projects at the Environmental Protection Agency

Resetting Our Future
Long Haul COVID: A Survivor's Guide:
Transform Your Pain & Find Your Way Forward
Dr. Joseph J. Trunzo, Professor of Psychology and Department
Chair at Bryant University, and Julie Luongo,
author of *The Hard Way*

SMART Futures for a Flourishing World
A Paradigm Shift for Achieving Global Sustainability
Dr. Claire Nelson, Chief Visionary Officer and Lead Futurist,
The Futures Forum

Rebalance
How Women Lead, Parent, Partner and Thrive
Monica Brand Engel, Lisa Neuberger Fernandez, and Wendy
Jagerson Teleki

Resetting the Table
Nicole Civita, Vice President of Strategic Initiatives at Sterling
College, Ethics Transformation in Food Systems, and Michelle
Auerbach

Unquenchable Thirst
How Water Rules the World and How Humans Rule Water
Luke Wilson and Alexandra Campbell-Ferrari, Co-Founders of
the Center for Water Security and Cooperation

www.ResettingOurFuture.com

I come as one, but I stand as ten thousand.
— Maya Angelou

To those whose passion, strength, courage and authenticity
have inspired us to find our voices.

Introduction

Life in the Balance

We will be more successful in all of our endeavors if we can let go of the habit of running all the time, and take little pauses to relax and re-center ourselves. And we'll also have a lot more joy in living.
–Thich Nhat Hanh

This book is inspired by a decade-long conversation between a fierce tribe of women, all of whom are in high octane jobs in social impact careers striving to make a difference as leaders, mothers, spouses, daughters, friends, neighbors and citizens. We work across a broad range of society's biggest challenges: women's economic empowerment, increasing corporate environmental responsibility, sparking social innovation, financial inclusion of the poorest around the world, legal justice, immigrant rights, national security and peace-building among others.

The first Friday of every month until COVID-19 hit, a dozen or so of us would get together at a cozy restaurant a few blocks from the White House for lunch, inspiration and allyship. At a table intimate enough to hear each other over the lunchtime din, we had wide-ranging, 360-degree conversations that left nothing unexplored: global challenges, workplace dramas, childcare traumas, health crises, societal upheavals and celebrations big and small – everything was on the menu.

We formed this group in 2010 and called it Thrive, well before Arianna Huffington wrote her excellent book by the same name. The group was created to tap the wisdom of our crowd to help each other navigate the many parts of our busy lives with purpose, confidence and foresight – and keep our humor and sanity while doing it. We were not titans of industry, political leaders or celebrities, and, like most working women, we did not aim to be. We were purpose-driven leaders in different sectors, with different stories, who shared an ambition to have a positive impact on society through our work. Equally important, we had children who we wanted to be happy and confident. We sought to rebalance our lives – to be in harmony with our spouses, our friends, our parents, our work, our own bodies and minds. We were eager to be a force for good in our communities and the world around us. Yet there are only so many hours in the day. Though the topics we discussed are varied, the perennial question was always there: is it possible to do it all well or does something have to give? There is no simple answer, but by sharing our trials, tribulations, regrets and sometimes wisdom, these discussions emboldened each of us to forge the path that is right for us.

As founding members of Thrive, the three of us had long felt that the insights of these conversations were powerful and worth sharing. There were so many Aha! moments in our discussions over the course of a decade. We grappled with how to trust our intuition and establish boundaries, how to listen with empathy and speak with conviction, how to stay true to our purpose and keep a growth mindset, and how to make room for joy and celebration in our busy lives. We knew so many other women our age who had similar aspirations and thought they might see themselves in some of our stories. We knew younger women, early in their careers, who were looking for examples of how to design their lives for good. And we knew men who also struggled to find balance but were often not privy to groups and conversations where such issues were discussed. This is why, as the world was shutting down in the early days of COVID-19, we decided to take advantage of the pause and share these insights in a book.

In addition to our Thrive meetings, we three authors were in the habit of walking and talking on Sunday mornings, a tradition that persisted during COVID-19, but suddenly with face masks and six feet between us. Our walk and talks helped us get perspective, dig deeper into the themes that arose in our monthly Thrive lunches, and find pathways to action. Over the years, our walk and talks have seen us through the raising of six children into their teenage years, important milestones with our spouses and communities, and career progressions, the latest of which include the launch of Monica's venture capital fund, Wendy's appointment to lead a global initiative to support women entrepreneurs, and Lisa's promotion to Managing Director in corporate citizenship innovation at a leading professional services firm.

As COVID-19 took hold, our conversations seemed to become even more essential. The pace of change in our personal and professional lives – and the world as we knew it – was difficult to process. The disruptions of 2020 were unfathomable. There were themes that we had been discussing for years, but COVID-19 gave them new urgency: How do we balance our care for our families, our communities and ourselves with our passion for social impact through work? What does success look like as the world of work changes? How do our children learn and grow through hardship? How should we show up for partners, friends and parents who are struggling? How do we understand our privileges and use them to combat inequality? How do we think about our own health and wellbeing as we age? As we walked and talked and wrote, we found that the pandemic was helping us get new, sometimes liberating perspectives on old challenges. We wrote the final words of this book the week that we were each finally double vaccinated against the virus. In other words, in the time it took us to write this book, the world changed forever, and so did we.

Full circle living

A touchstone for us was an exercise we simply called "the

wheel." Once or twice a year, pre-COVID-19, the Thrive women carved out time for a longer "flash" retreat, finding time by leaving work a few hours early and coming home a few hours late. We often kicked off with "the wheel," a well-known coaching tool shared with us by one of our early Thrive members. Anyone can create a wheel anytime. All it takes is a blank piece of paper and a pen. You draw a circle and divide it into as many slices as you need to represent the important areas of your life. Then you shade each slice from the center out, stopping at a point which represents how satisfied you are with that part of your life, and leaving white space from there to the edge to represent the work still to be done. The white space in each of the slices becomes the subject of the retreat.

The most common question newcomers ask about the wheel is what does the edge represent? If there were a single Thrive philosophy, it could be found in the answer. Getting to the edge is not about attaining some abstract ideal, someone else's expectation of what it means to be the perfect mother, friend, leader, partner, etc. It represents where we personally would like to be at that moment, all things considered. Looking to get in the best shape of your life and run a marathon? Welcome to the edge of the wheel. Know that we'd be happy just to walk around the neighborhood a few times a week? That works, too. After drawing wheels for many years in a row, we have seen how our aspirations for each slice on the wheel can wax and wane. Some years we feel confident that we are doing all we can for our kids and want to push harder at work, sometimes it is the opposite. Other years we may face a yawning white space when it comes to a partner or aging parents. We learn and adjust. From one year to the next, entire slices get taken out or added.

From this exercise, we have learned that we are not interested in "having it all" all of the time. Rather, we seek to shape our lives in intentional and innovative ways that let us focus on the right things at the right times to balance all the dimensions of our lives. We relish our agency and our ability to actively design the lives we want to lead notwithstanding the constraints we naturally face. This includes how we show up as mothers, leaders, partners and citizens. We are each responsible for defining which slices are in our own wheels, celebrating what is working and deciding what needs our attention. And when change happens, as it inevitably does, we can redraw the wheel and reset our intentions.

Re-drawing the circle post-COVID-19

For ten years, we drew and redrew our own wheels each year, adjusting them along the way. Then COVID-19 hit and the world turned upside down. With astonishing speed, we let go of old ways of working and adopted new technologies and approaches to work, family and community-building. Priorities shifted. Our lives became less frenetic but no less stressful. More than just disrupting our own lives, the pandemic laid bare the dramatic inequalities in our society. Fissures grew into Grand Canyons overnight. Kids without wi-fi at home woke up without access to school. Jobs that were supposed to be safe from automation disappeared with sudden, unprecedented shutdowns. Underlying socio-economic and health inequalities had deadly consequences. For those of us in jobs focused on driving positive change in society, the crisis elevated the urgency of that work. Watching the massive disruptions taking hold, we started to see more clearly the interdependencies between our work, our family, our health and our communities.

We were inspired to reimagine a new way forward with greater balance and purpose in our lives. We found ourselves saying things like: "This is the first time in 25 years I have gone for months without a business trip and I kind of like it," "My job has become my part-time gig now that caring for kids and parents has become full-time," and "I'm not going back to the way it was." Rather than reverting to the old ways of work after the pandemic, we have resolved to use this experience to reset our expectations, rethink our work and home lives, and re-imagine ways to find a more perfect harmony between our work, families and personal wellbeing.

What to expect from this book

We are each in the midst of a journey with many unexpected twists and turns and no simple answers. This book shares some of the experiences and insightful conversations that have helped us along the way. We hope these will resonate and maybe even inspire the men and women who read this book who are looking to find fulfillment and happiness in their busy lives.

We have organized this book as we tend to organize the wheel, in four sections focused on: **Work, Family, Self,** and **Community**. Within each section are three chapters covering key issues we grapple with within each of those themes.

- In the *Work* section we look at building purpose-driven careers, leading at work and finding flexibility at work to promote balance.
- In the *Family* section we look at how we parent and how we partner with presence and intentionality, and how we manage the guilt that working mothers always grapple with.
- In the *Self* section we look at finding a path to health, finding time for gratitude and celebration, and giving ourselves permission to let go.
- In the *Community* section we look at how we build support networks and friend groups that help us pull it all together, the communities that we invest in, and how to bring our authentic voices to create the world we want to see.

We have found that across the many areas of our lives, common themes emerge. These include the importance of using our voice with authenticity and conviction; the power of listening to our intuition and pausing; the art of setting boundaries and giving ourselves permission to find joy and care for ourselves; the importance of allies to achieving success and balance, and above all, the belief that we have agency to design the life to which we aspire.

In writing this book we have drawn on the stories, humor and wisdom of so many, and we hope that this book will carry inspiration to many more who may recognize themselves in our journeys. We are very conscious of and grateful for the options in our lives that were made possible by our upbringings, educational opportunities, career journeys and life partners. We realize that many of the choices we have made are not necessarily available to everyone who may read this book. In reflecting on how to frame the insights we share here, we do not mean to diminish or oversimplify the real constraints many women in diverse circumstances face every day. We hope that the message of taking control of the things we can, getting clear on what is most important today, and laying the foundations to grasp future opportunities is one that will resonate with our readers.

Section I

Leading Differently at Work

We start this book with the section on work not because it is the most important part of our lives. We begin with work because for most of the Thrive women, including the three of us, we were professionals first. Before we met our husbands, before our lives were transformed by our children, and before we put down roots, we had launched our careers. Work is an important part of who we are. We have found our way to purpose-driven jobs we love, where we believe we can make a difference. We find purpose through our work and share an optimistic view that we can influence the world around us to make it a better place. We are ambitious – not so much to garner titles or accolades; but to have an impact on what we care about through our work and to feel respected, accomplished, and fulfilled from applying ourselves in this way. But it's not always the easy path we've chosen. We are constantly questioning: Am I staying true to my passion and purpose in my career? Am I doing my best to influence change in and through my organization and the world? Am I giving the right amount of myself to work compared to the other parts of my life that are important? Am I doing enough? Thrive has helped us find ways to answer these questions with intentionality.

Designing Careers with Purpose

Forget about the fast lane. If you really want to fly, harness our power to our passion. Honor our calling. Everybody has one. Trust our heart, and success will come to you.

—Oprah Winfrey

"Imagine you're in the desert suffering from heat stroke and dehydration. Do you (A) try to get water out of a cactus and risk getting spines stuck in our hand (turn to page 15)? Or (B) pick a succulent which could easily quench our thirst as long as you don't pick the rare poisonous ones (turn to page 35)? It's up to you." Lisa's favorite childhood books were from a series called *Choose Our Own Adventure*. These books, now collectors' items, allow the reader to choose how the story will evolve and, ultimately, how it will end. Lisa remembers curling up on a comfortable pink polka dot chair by her bedroom window on hot Texas afternoons, finding different paths as she read the books over and over again. She loved the anticipation of what was just around the corner and the fun of being able to control the storyline. A new Netflix series called *Wild vs. You* has the same premise and was a COVID-19 favorite for her family. Their debates over whether to send the main character down the riskier path – with the possibility of great rewards or impending doom – or the more secure and comfortable path, were lively and revealing.

We think of our own careers like a "Choose Our Own Adventure" journey. Each of us has pursued careers that give us a sense of purpose, guided by a north star that drives us. Our paths have had many twists and turns, with many fateful choices. We have often chosen to take the roads less traveled. Indeed, our most defining and ultimately rewarding career moments have been when we decided to pursue – or create –

opportunities that we were passionate about even though they were risky or unconventional. Making those decisions with intentionality from the start has helped us build careers that enabled us to support our families and wake up excited and grateful to go to work each day.

Finding our purpose at work and pursuing it with conviction has not always been easy. Many of us were sometimes tempted by gilded paths taken by our fellow graduates or attracted to the security and predictability of pursuing a well-oiled, fast track to advancement. At times, we faced self-doubt or family disapproval when we made choices defined by deeper purpose rather than societal expectations. When we followed our hearts and took risks, we often worried that they would be heart-over-head blunders. But we've found that following our passion is not destined to make us aimless dreamers as long as we are purposeful in how we go about it. Over twenty years plus, we have seen how important it is to find jobs that align with our interests and that we can help shape with allies who understood our intentions and saw our potential. Even when our risky decisions didn't pan out, we learned from them. Our experience has only built our resilience and strengthened our resolve. We have learned the importance of taking risks, setting our compass, asking for what we want, never giving up, and building allies.

What could go *right*? the rewards of risk taking

It may seem counterintuitive, but when we look back at our most important career decisions, we see that our riskiest decisions were often our best decisions. In Wendy's case, the most fateful decision she took was coming out of college in 1990. She had a vague notion that she wanted to "make a difference" and "do something international" but beyond that, things were fuzzy. Over the years, she had interned in Congress, at the UN, and at a think tank, all of which had mostly helped her understand what she *didn't* want to do. Her Bachelor's degree in international relations and some basic Russian skills from Occidental College also didn't seem to be opening any doors. Six months out, she was working at the deli down the street from her mother's house and volunteering for a newsletter for Russian women. When she heard about a women's conference in the collapsing Soviet Union, she and a friend wrangled invites and ten-day visas to attend the event. Wendy bought a one-way ticket and packed for a three-month trip. Ultimately, one week would turn into four years living through the dissolution of the USSR in what would become independent Ukraine and helping to privatize and transform their private sector. Her rash decision to just pick up and go to a rapidly collapsing empire would ultimately lead her to two top graduate schools and a career in the World Bank Group, not to mention meeting her husband and all the goodness that followed.

Was there fear and uncertainty when she boarded the plane to Moscow with her one-week visa, $500 in her pocket and no roadmap? Indeed. But the risks seemed worth the potential rewards, particularly at a time when the stakes were still low for her. Alternatively, what would have happened if Wendy had gotten an entry-level job at a corporation or NGO out of college? Who knows? But by hopping on that plane, she gained experience that was priceless and opened doors for many, many years. In fact, that one decision in many ways defined her choices for the rest of her life.

Stay tuned to true north

In Wendy's case, her inner compass directed her towards international development, leveraging her skills to focus on small business development around the world. Not all Thrive women discovered where they wanted to build their careers so early on; but they all locked into their north star and used it as a guide to create opportunities. For us, clarifying true north means reflecting on how we define success for ourselves. Asking ourselves the questions: What motivates me? What do I value most? This notion of a self-defined true north is central to the wheel exercise. We have found by trial and error that the more our wheels contain slices that are motivated intrinsically by our own values, the more satisfied we ultimately are. Conversely, the more we let ourselves be driven by external motivators – such as climbing a corporate ladder or living up to a parent, spouse, employer or peer's expectations – the less satisfying it is to reach that goal.

Monica graduated from Stanford Business School in the late 1990s, at the height of the internet boom. Most classmates were focused on staying in Silicon Valley, enticed, as she was, by its entrepreneurial ethos, stunning weather and seemingly boundless opportunities. But she had her sights set on working abroad, influenced strongly by her parents – a Peruvian mother who spoke limited English when she came to the US, and her father who had been a Peace Corps volunteer and later pursued an MBA and corporate career in New York. She was intent on combining her passion for entrepreneurship and Latina roots by working in business overseas with some kind of development angle. Though it didn't check all of her boxes, an offer to work for McKinsey in South Africa seemed compelling. The Truth and Reconciliation commissions, launched following Nelson Mandela's inspiring ascendancy from prison to president, were airing on campus: it felt like a sign. Moreover, she had borrowed significantly to go to business school, and the company would pay for her graduate loans and provide her an undeniable pedigree. She took the job and flew to Johannesburg.

As Monica drove through the Johannesburg suburbs with the corporate relocation team, she started to have misgivings. She realized there was a disconnect when she asked to see more diverse neighborhoods and the HR manager was not encouraging. At the same time, she was hearing exciting things about the nascent entrepreneurial ecosystem in South Africa. It began to dawn on Monica that her heart was not in the corporate consulting world. As she agonized, she confided in her friend Linda Rottenberg who was also about to embark on her own groundbreaking social enterprise called Endeavor. Linda asked Monica a question she will never forget: "Do you really need another stamp [of approval] on your forehead, Monica?" The question helped filter out the extraneous considerations of money and prestige that a top consulting firm would provide, and refocused Monica on her true north. In the end, she decided to take a fellowship to work at a venture capital firm in Cape Town focused on previously disadvantaged entrepreneurs. While the decision was complicated, she knew that she needed to forge her career based on the elements that were priorities for her: development finance, emerging markets, innovation and entrepreneurship. Monica's choice enabled her to chart a career focused on bringing product innovation and entrepreneurial finance to the poorest of the world with ACCION, one of the leading global microfinance players. It later led to the creation of venture capital fund Quona Capital which invests in technologies that drive financial inclusion in emerging markets ("fintech for inclusion"), crystalizing those early dreams.

Could Monica have "paid her dues" in a brand name firm and then come back to the development world in a second act? We've seen people make this transition successfully. However, we have seen many more who never make it to the second act for one reason or another, and we ask ourselves, why postpone a shot at fulfillment? Indeed, fulfillment is like finance: great rewards accrue to those willing to take the risk.

Aligning profits and purpose

Many Thrive women have built their careers in well-established organizations and have found ways to innovate and forge new paths from within. They are *intra*preneurs or corporate changemakers, catalytic thinkers who spur innovation from within an organization rather than from the outside. Many of our career moves have come about because we saw an opportunity or problem, identified a solution, and found a way to lead implementing it that leveraged the formidable assets of the organizations that employ us.

Upon completing a joint MBA and Masters in foreign affairs in 2000, Lisa had an offer to return to the New York City office of Accenture, the global, professional services company she worked at before graduate school that was sponsoring her studies. She interviewed with a number of NGOs and then realized that she wanted to return to consulting but transfer her offer to San Francisco. After a decade living on the East Coast, she was eager to dive into the more "zen-like" Northern California way of life and realize a vision she was developing with a fellow changemaker. Their idea was to combine the know-how of her company's talented professionals as volunteer coaches with the time and smarts of business school students who would obtain course credit for their work. Together the teams would deliver valuable services to local nonprofit organizations who could benefit from the strategic advice. This innovative twist on a *pro bono* consulting model was designed to bring to life the positive role that business could play in society.

Her experience pitching the idea to the head of the San Francisco office was illuminating. As Lisa made her case, she was acutely aware that she was a freshly minted MBA making an unsolicited proposal to one of the company's senior Managing Directors. Not to mention that the proposal would invest the company's resources with no immediate financial return in sight – albeit with the promise of improving outcomes for nonprofits and creating longer term corporate value. She had taken the first two essential steps to becoming a social intrapreneur. She had identified an innovative solution and she had gathered up the courage to ask for the authority and resources to implement it. She held her breath while she waited for his response, which has never left her. The San Francisco leader didn't say yes. And he didn't say no. What he said instead was, "Tell me the business case and I'll consider it." He posed three questions:

- What's the value proposition? Why is this relevant to our clients?
- Why now? What's the burning platform?
- Why you? Assuming this was a good idea with a strong value case, why are you uniquely suited to take this idea from vision to reality?

These three simple questions struck a chord deep in Lisa as she saw them as a kind of treasure map for an intrapreneur. She was ready and responded with details and confidence. She explained how the initiative would help the firm acquire and retain talent, make a statement about the company's responsibilities beyond the bottom line, and bolster the leader's legacy. Her proposal was accepted and launched an important chapter in her career.

The exchange taught Lisa a valuable lesson in how to chart our own adventure when others need to buy into it. A changemaker who is going to drive lasting change in an organization needs to start with a deep understanding of all of her stakeholders: What motivates them? What do they need? What do they expect? How do they define success? By prompting her to articulate a business case that would address value to a whole host of stakeholders, the San Francisco leader was inviting her to get out of her head and into theirs. Lisa had to walk in his shoes and understand his perspective – how would he make the business case to his colleagues? She was hooked, and has applied this lesson countless times when inventing and pitching social innovations at the company in the twenty years since.

Seeing this pattern play out in our different organizations, we have learned to not be afraid to envision that better future and to take the initiative to make it happen, ask for what we think is important, and come prepared to make our case. This conviction is crucial whether asking for a raise or a promotion, or suggesting the creation of a new project, product or initiative. We may not get everything we ask for, but we just might – and we may also get things that we never asked for. The power of asking is that we are creating a new opportunity that we are passionate about and that will benefit from our unique skills and perspective.

Growth mindset in the driver's seat

Though we have progressed and attained titles, our careers have not taken linear paths. Sometimes we have taken clear steps up and sometimes our career moves have taken us sideways. But what has been consistent is that we have always pursued opportunities where we could learn and that inspired us. We define professional success along two dimensions, which in turn have driven our career choices: first, having a measurable impact on our world in ways that we found meaningful, starting with our inner circle and rippling out to society at large; and second, learning and building new skills at each step in our careers. In some cases, it is this appetite for growth and learning that is the biggest motivator.

At each decision point, it is important to ask which path will provide the greatest opportunity to learn, grow, and grapple with challenges we have not seen before. Sometimes the growth opportunity is as straightforward as becoming a better public speaker or team leader, other times it is more complex, like learning how to manage politically fraught stakeholder groups or lead an organization through a tricky transition. When we lean into these growth opportunities, we are inevitably happier and more confident that we have made the right decisions.

Lisa realized how important personal growth and intrinsic goals were when she became a Managing Director at the company where she has worked since graduating from college. What surprised her was how short-lived the euphoria was after so many years of dreaming and working hard to reach the highest rank at her company. It felt like a roller-coaster ride, with a tremendous high after getting the promotion, followed by a few months of feeling inexplicably let down. She started to feel motivated and in the flow again only months later once she identified how her new role could be a platform to have an even greater impact at her organization and in her community in uncharted ways. She also started to focus more on setting her own personal goals such as learning how to cross-country ski and to sing jazz. It was only then that the life lesson really hit home. While it was rewarding to have the recognition and get a raise, what truly motivated her and gave her the most satisfaction had not changed: having an impact and growing as an individual.

The importance of allies

Building a career as a successful change maker, whether within a big organization or as an entrepreneur, one needs allies. Change is hard. Change breeds resistance. Even the most powerful leaders cannot effect change without bringing others along. In our Thrive discussions, so many conversations about our aspirations and challenges end up coming back to: Who are your allies? Who has got your back and who will advocate for you? Sometimes, we act as allies for each other, but more often we talk about how to build and cultivate relationships with key allies where we work. Peers, team members, collaborators, mentors, more senior leaders and sometimes random acquaintances all can become powerful allies. We have even observed the strange and powerful alchemy when an adversary is turned into an ally.

We can never know in advance where our path will take us or who we may meet along the way, but at each stage in our career, someone from our past may be the ally that we most need. When Wendy was a young gun working on privatization in Ukraine, she crossed paths with a similar team in Moscow, sharing wild stories about the craziness of post-Soviet economic reform. Years later, she was paired in a mentoring program with one of the staff who had worked in Russia and had become a successful manager and a mother of three. While the mentoring program was short-lived, they kept in touch informally after that, though they had little opportunity to interact on projects. Fifteen years later, that woman had risen to the top of the Corporation and was the one to call Wendy to ask if she would be interested in taking on a big new initiative to support women entrepreneurs around the world.

Lisa had a similar experience. When she first moved to Washington, DC, a mentor thoughtfully introduced her to a senior leader also new to the area. They met for lunch and soon found an opportunity to collaborate on creating a job training program for foster youth with one of the company's clients. This gave Lisa a chance to build a relationship and demonstrate her ability to make an impact. Years later, when she was up for Managing Director, the same senior lawyer had taken on a new role that put her in the position to champion her promotion. In both of these cases, the opportunities would not have been possible without the support of these leaders, yet their impressions and confidence to help advance their careers were only possible because of relationships forged, almost incidentally, years before.

Choosing our own (career) adventures can introduce uncertainty. Our careers can progress in a steady, well-plotted path, or can shift suddenly with a phone call or chance meeting in an elevator. Sometimes we get what we want, and sometimes things don't go our way. Indeed, at the Thrive table, we've celebrated decisions that tipped our way but we've also commiserated over those that did not. We don't always get to choose, but we can attest to the fact that luck favors the prepared when it comes to our careers. Each conversation, each deliverable, can become a factor in our career progression. If we demonstrate integrity, ingenuity, a growth mindset and hold fast to our values, we are more prepared to make that leap. If we are following our purpose and our passion, these characteristics are more likely to shine through in our work. Then, when the right job opens up, or inspiration sparks, we have the allies, trust and confidence of decision makers to let us choose our next adventure.

A career is a journey. It's a marathon, not a sprint. The sooner we start treating our journeys like a "choose our own adventure," where we are sitting in the driver's seat, the sooner we can start enjoying the ride and the more meaning and fulfillment we will find along the way.

Lead Different as Strong, Authentic, Effective Managers

When we women grant ourselves permission to live as our truest selves, we automatically grant others around us to do the same.
—Glennon Doyle

The situation in the room was tense. Senior government officials were being grilled by a Cabinet member on a matter of national urgency, and it was not going well. One after another, the senior officials in the room were being eviscerated for bumbling through their answers to the Secretary's questions. The most junior person, and the only female in the room, was a member of Thrive. With her superiors fumbling, she began to speak up. She responded to the rapid-fire questions with her own analysis of the situation, supporting her seniors' positions where she could and being careful not to highlight their errors. Relieved to be getting some answers, the Secretary zeroed in on her. She held steady and conveyed the facts and her analysis. With her calm, calibrated manner and clear expertise, she impressed everyone in the room. But the moment she credits with gaining the trust of the Secretary was when he finally asked her a question that she did not have good intelligence on and she said: "I don't know; let me research the answer and get back to you." Unlike the scornful look he had given her seniors, he thanked her for her insights and said he looked forward to getting her further advice on this topic.

Standing on the shoulder (pads) of others

This story was shared as Thrive members were reflecting on role models who had shaped their leadership style. The Thrive women entered the workforce in the 1990s – in a growing economy, full of optimism. There were women making strides in different sectors. In government, Madeleine Albright and Janet Reno became powerful Cabinet members and Hillary

Clinton took on substantive policy issues as First Lady – inspiring millions in her declaration that "Women's Rights are Human Rights" at the World Conference on Women in Beijing.[2] Meg Whitman and Carly Fiorina entered the ranks of Fortune 500 CEOs, innovating and disrupting in the traditionally male technology sector. In the media, Katharine Graham, Oprah Winfrey and Martha Stewart became business moguls in their own rights. The movie *Working Girl* and TV series *Murphy Brown* embodied the new narrative about women in leadership, showing how women could compete with men and succeed.

Yet, much of this narrative focused on how women, to lead, needed to be more like men, with pantsuits and shoulder pads just being the tip of the iceberg. In business school we learned to play golf, smoke cigars, and compete to win. While the dominant advice was that women needed to be more like men in the workplace, we also saw the reality that women were often judged harshly when they took this advice. We saw women leaders being viciously attacked for being too tough (Janet Reno, Carly Fiorina), and being phony (Hillary Clinton, Martha Stewart). If ambition came at a high price for all of these pioneers, it was even more complicated for those who were also mothers. Many of these pioneers either had no children (Oprah Winfrey, Janet Reno) or their children had grown by the time they became prominent public figures in their own right (Madeleine Albright, Katherine Graham). Those who tried to show that the two could be balanced were eviscerated – Hilary Clinton and Murphy Brown became part of the culture wars when they did.[3] Even as recently as 2012, Marisa Meyer was publicly shamed as she tried to navigate running Yahoo while having a newborn.

In many ways, we have been the beneficiaries of those who called out and ended blatantly discriminatory practices in our workplaces, and by and large we feel we have faced a more balanced playing field than our mothers and grandmothers did.

Lisa recalls a story her beloved grandmother often recounted to explain how much change she witnessed in her lifetime. As the only woman on her 1939 Oklahoma City high school debate team to win the US national tournament to much pride and fanfare, her grandmother never forgot how her cherished coach reacted to her announcement that she wanted to go to Law School. Unlike the encouragement given her teammates, he said, "Oh honey, that's a terribly hard row to hoe for a gal." Her grandmother never finished college but later became an entrepreneur translating her love of art, design, and helping people into a successful decorating business. To her very last days, she continued to recite poems eloquently and to encourage her daughters and grandchildren to embrace and cultivate their own voices and entrepreneurial spirits – and to never let anyone narrow their ambitions.

Wendy's father was a pioneering consultant advising Fortune 500 clients on the new equal employment laws in the 1970s. She recalls looking through his consulting materials that explained why it was not okay for a manager to pat his secretaries' behinds or to fire a woman when she got married. Thankfully, those times are mostly behind us. But recently there has been a flood of research on implicit bias that women face at work, giving a name to the more subtle challenges and "microaggressions" that are sometimes hard to decipher.[4] Research looking at why so few women founders get venture capital financing, has shown how venture investors ask women founders more negative questions than male founders, forcing them to focus their limited pitch time on the downside risks their firms face, while men could focus more on their (generally over-confident) assessment of their business potential.[5] Other research has shown that male Supreme Court justices interrupt their female colleagues three times more frequently than their male colleagues, regardless of seniority or political affiliations. Seeing evidence of these implicit biases in black and white is validating, gives us pause, and helps us address them in our daily interactions with our colleagues, not to mention our children, husbands and others.

Embracing our own leadership paths

In our careers, we have aspired to move beyond the bifurcated stereotypes of women at work needing to be either relentlessly pleasant and accommodating or aggressively competitive. We find ourselves wanting to define our own models of success that draw on our deep-rooted instincts to feel, foster inquiry, build bridges, and encourage colleagues to bring their whole selves to work. We know vulnerability, relationships and psychological safety are not necessarily "female" traits, just as aggressiveness, assertiveness and firm handshakes are not necessarily male. The more we are able to master and toggle between these skills, the better able we are to foster excellence in our work. And we aim to pass this on to the next generation as our predecessors passed on their legacy to us. If it was true for us that "we teach boys to take risks and girls to be good," we want our daughters and sons to know that they can – and should – do both.[12]

The role models and cautionary tales from our past have helped us as we have sought to navigate our careers with our own leadership style. We are buoyed by our own experiences as well as a raft of new research showing that we can contribute on our own terms in the workplace. Research published in the Harvard Business Review shows that women outscore men on 17 of the 19 capabilities that differentiate excellent leaders from average or poor ones.[6] Google research on high-performing teams has shown that the features most predictive of team success were psychological safety, dependability, structure and clarity, meaning and impact.[7] Like plants that bend toward the light, people thrive in work spaces that are encouraging, caring and supportive. With data like this, there is a strong case to be made that the future of leadership could well be female.

In our thirst for insights on how to lead better, we have

found the traditional management literature helpful, but not enough. One book that profiled successful women leaders only mentioned their children once, noting how helpful it was that one of the women sent her children to boarding school. Others rely too much on the "woman as nurturer" stereotype.

We have been inspired to find a growing group of authors with new perspectives on how to balance the personal with the professional, the assertive with the compassionate, the hard-driver tendency with the people-pleaser. Sheryl Sandberg encouraged us to *lean in* to our professional careers in her book of the same title; but to do so with authenticity and curiosity.[8] Anne-Marie Slaughter pointed out the systemic barriers women need to overcome when trying to balance work and life.[9] Kim Scott, an executive coach and author of *Radical Candor* showed us how the combination of "caring personally while challenging directly" creates the kind of feedback loops that make teams succeed.[10] Esther Perel, a famed couples therapist whose work with the VC fund First Round Capital spawned the *How's Work* podcast, illuminated how the way people "show up" in personal relationships applies in the workplace. And Brene Brown introduced her now famous research on vulnerability and empathy as an untapped source of power and leadership strength.[11]

Three levels of leadership: a new ladder to climb

So, what do these insights have to teach us about how to show up and succeed at work in authentic, holistic ways? In years of conversation helping each other get through difficult work situations and finding pathways to success, a certain level of pattern recognition has kicked in. What has emerged is an understanding that our struggles to lead take place at three levels, with each level requiring different skills and awareness. The first level is the heads-down focus on mastering one's trade, self-regulating and earning trust, which ultimately provides degrees of freedom to maneuver. The second level is mastering your relationship with others, leading a team and managing up. The final level is when we can begin to influence the rules of the game and affect systems change that will drive better outcomes on a broader scale. Though our early careers are defined by level-one mastery, and we tend to gain the broader perspective that level-three requires as we mature, we are testing and building the skills at each level all the time. We are all still as much on the path of personal mastery, as we are learning how to effect systems change. Through it all, we are learning as we go. Some of the insights we've gathered related to each level are described below.

Level 1: Master our trade – Tap into superpowers and core strength

There is no substitute for competence. Facing down the Secretary's withering questions was the start of a rapid and unconventional career progression for that Thrive member. She had been thrust into a stretch assignment where she quickly had to get up to speed while managing up and across. She immediately immersed herself in the topic and made sure she was over-prepared for briefings with the executive decision makers, earning herself a reputation for being a reliable source of intelligence and level-headed analysis. She inspired confidence by also admitting what she didn't know and conscientiously addressing those gaps in her follow-ups. Her dogged hard work paid off when it came time for the Secretary to consider a replacement for her boss. The Secretary insisted on having her fill the position, notwithstanding considerable pressure to place a political appointee in that role.

Cultivate superpowers

We have found that the first step in establishing oneself as a powerhouse in the workplace is to understand and cultivate one's strengths. Whether we are naturally good at analysis, modeling, communicating, networking, innovating or just getting things done, making sure we are demonstrating that skill set to others is critical. We all spent the first years in our careers becoming known for what we do well; sometimes others saw what those superpowers were even before we recognized them in ourselves. When we are passionate about what we are doing, finding and demonstrating our strengths comes more naturally.

Monica always felt her early successes came from working hard to understand her clients, collaborating with others to problem solve, and reliably delivering. Her passion to address financial inclusion challenges, and curiosity about the limits of microfinance, drove her to launch a business unit focused on product innovation.[13] She had as many setbacks as victories, and often faced resistance to change. Inspired by stories of the failures, resilience and resurgence of tech leaders explored in Walter Isaacson's well-known book *The Innovators*, she persisted.[14] She approached challenges as learning opportunities, which made the long hours and a peripatetic schedule more enjoyable than exhausting. Instead of giving up, she built her experience and credibility by getting involved operationally in a number of new product launches, researching successful models, building a team and pilot testing new ideas. Launching new products with one of her company's most successful microfinance partners, she was able to earn the trust that would ultimately enable her to expand her areas of responsibility. This culminated in managing the company's first fintech fund.

In a similar way, starting early in her career, Lisa was motivated to find innovative ways to channel corporate resources to tackle societal challenges. In one instance, she patented a new way of measuring the social ROI of government spending. More recently, she inspired her team to bring together thousands of employees, corporates, startups and NGO experts for an innovation challenge to try to turn the tide on climate change.

Through such initiatives, she built a reputation as someone who could build a vision and create innovative ways to get people to take on socially relevant causes in ways that were empowering, built a sense of common purpose, and were good for business.

There is no substitute for performance, so the sooner we discover what we do best and tap that, the easier things become. When we find our zone, the place where work is a pleasure, that is when we are most likely to succeed at being both passionate about and highly effective in our jobs.

Own our strengths

Finding our strengths is an essential skill, yet even when we find our superpower and knock it out of the park time and again, it is not necessarily enough to get us where we want to go. We can sabotage our best efforts when we don't stand up for ourselves and act as our own champion. Self-efficacy and its corollary self-promotion are critical at this level.

One Thrive member described an experience early in her career, when she got consistently great performance reviews but was repeatedly passed up for a promotion. She felt frustrated and hurt, but she didn't truly understand what had happened until a senior woman in her company stepped into her office and closed the door. "Listen," she said, "I'm going to explain something to you. Nobody is going to come in here and put a tiara on our head." The implication was clear: technical competence would only get you so far; it's up to you to make sure your excellence is noticed, recognized and rewarded. While we don't advocate walking around the office in a tiara, or its metaphorical equivalent, it is important to proactively seek opportunities to demonstrate how you can deliver at the next level, to be bold and ask for the things you want such as a promotion, and to find allies who will help you achieve your goals.

Research shows that women tend to be more critical of their own skills than men are and, accordingly, to self-promote less.[15]

A familiar trap that keeps many women (and some men) from promoting themselves is the "imposter syndrome," or doubting one's ability to perform in a job. While it is important to be aware of and address weaknesses, many women too often buy into a narrative that defines them by the gaps in their resume or the skills that have yet to be mastered. When we've let the doubting voices in our heads overshadow the cheerleaders, we've become uncomfortable tooting our own horns and stepping up to the plate, afraid of failure.

With the doubting voices blaring, Lisa recalls receiving and immediately shelving Sheryl Sandberg's iconic book *Lean In*, too anxious about whether she had what it takes to lean into her career and ask for a promotion. When she finally was ready to dust it off years later, she found inspiration in Sandburg's insistence that we deserve and need to take a seat at the table – sometimes quite literally. It helped Lisa realize that it's one thing to have the competence to merit a promotion and quite another to have the confidence to step up, ask for it, prove that you're ready for it, and own the outcome.

Wendy had a similar experience typical for many women when she was asked to consider a new position. Her immediate reaction was "I could never do that job." While she knew the technical side of the work hands down, she had never been involved in the kind of high-level stakeholder management that the job would entail. After consulting with the Thrive tribe and examining her discomfort head on, her perspective flipped. The job would be a perfect opportunity to showcase formidable technical strengths, while posing a great learning opportunity on the stakeholder management side. If she went into the experience with a structured approach to building this new skill set, she became confident that she would be a great fit for the job and learn a lot doing it. This reframing became a theme in our Thrive group: rather than see a career opportunity as a bridge too far to cross, it is a chance to apply what we do well and build new skills along the way.

Setting boundaries

Level 1 leadership is also about building the self-awareness to know what your red lines are, and being assertive enough to enforce them. Early in our careers, it can be hard to say no, whether to excessive work or toxic workplace behavior. Many of us saw our early career years as a sprint – working long hours, taking on more projects, building new skills as quickly as we could to build credibility, connections, and competencies. For those of us looking to have children, fitting as much in before we became mothers seemed important. We had a hard time setting boundaries. But as we gained responsibilities and our lives became more complex, we needed to learn the skill of setting boundaries: How much work would we take on? What limits did we need to set on our working hours? And what were our red lines around bullying behavior at work? It can be hard to be confident in what we deserve, quiet the voices of doubt, and be honest with others about what we need, even if it is not what they want to hear.

We have all had situations where a demanding boss or client floods us with strongly worded emails, makes seemingly coded comments, or stonewalls us. What we have found is that while we may not control them, we do have control over how we react to them. In the face of ambiguous messages, we may jump to conclusions and think the worst. Sometimes it is an annoyance, and sometimes it becomes a radioactive element in our lives, permeating our day with tension. Often, the people pleaser comes out in us and we try to accommodate. Other times, we overreact. When we instead draw our own lines and are intentional and clear in our responses, we are at our best.

When emails were creating unwelcome stress in her life, Lisa found a creative way to manage her knee jerk reactions to seeing them pop into her email box. She noticed that when she read them with a defensive mindset, she would often take the messages too personally, feel defeated, and overreact. Brainstorming with another Thrive member, an idea popped up. What if she could put these "steaming hot" emails on hold in a special email folder? She jumped on the idea and created a dedicated email folder she called the "freezer." The idea of the "freezer" was to temporarily hold onto these emails to give them (and her) time to cool down. In the time the emails were chilling in the freezer, she could put them into perspective, find appropriate words for her response, and seek the advice of others in case she was missing something. It may have made her less prompt in her replies, but it paid off in terms of her ability to respond professionally, assertively, and constructively. Just the act of creating the folder with intentionality helped. The folder contains very few emails to this day as it seems that even creating the folder helped her rethink her habits and reframe her mindset.

Another Thrive member was on the lookout for her next job and was asked if she would be interested in running what she considered a dream project. The project was exciting, challenging and focused on something she was passionate about – hands down the perfect next step for her. She was thrilled when a Director she had worked with and respected asked her to take it on. The only problem was that to run the project she would have to work under a manager who by reputation and in her own experiences could be capricious. By this time, she had three children under five and had no interest in entering a toxic work situation. She wondered if she should take another job offer, with a great manager but on a project that she was not as excited about. Instead, she took a deep breath and told the Director that she would take the job, but only if she could report to him and not the manager. She explained why and also how she thought she could coordinate with the manager but be accountable to the Director. To his credit, he agreed. It wasn't always easy, but in the end, she forged a good relationship with the manager and built a successful program.

Learn how to self-regulate

Unfortunately, we're not always able to delay or avoid unpleasant situations – they happen every day, sometimes in open conflicts and other times through micro-aggressions. Learning how to self-regulate, assert our boundaries, while also modulating our responses is an art rather than a science. Whether insisting on a change in the tone of communications, enlisting allies to stand up to bullies, or sharing data and evidence with management, forceful responses to toxic behavior are sometimes needed. Other times, success truly is the best revenge.[16]

At one raucous lunch, we were talking about common situations where we had been talked down to, dismissed or gaslighted. As we commiserated, an attorney, a petite Latina with a youthful look, explained how she was often addressed dismissively in the courtroom which was totally inappropriate for her position. Not one to suffer fools, any number of handy retorts would naturally be on the tip of her tongue. Knowing, however, that she would prevail by focusing on her case, she had developed a mantra for these moments: "Don't say it, Susana... Don't say it, Susana..." She would focus on the case at hand, and when the comment had come from a colleague, she would take them head on in her own time. The image of her harnessing her emotions by silently repeating her mantra, while demonstrating why they underestimated her at their peril, made us laugh until we cried. "Don't say it, Susana" has now become a shorthand for us whenever we grapple with how to lay down boundaries with intentionality, courage and a little levity.

Level 2: Build thriving teams – Channel the pressure and bring out the potential of others

In *What Got You Here, Won't Get You There*, Marshall Goldsmith describes the step change that takes place when moving from being a great doer to being a great manager.[17] This is what we mean by Level 2 leadership, when we can no longer rely on our own work ethic, technical expertise and sound judgment alone to deliver results.

In many Thrive lunchtime conversations we talked about the challenges moving from Level 1 to Level 2, from being the person on the team in charge of the analysis to being the leader of the team. How to motivate others to identify problems and deliver solutions together. How to embrace our own authority, and also learn to delegate – a sometimes painful process of letting go just as we are being given greater accountability. How to find our individual style of coaching and mentoring others – not just telling people what to do but leading them to their own answers. And how to find allies to amplify our voices and challenge behaviors that make teams less effective.

Courage to let go

A core source of anxiety for Thrive women moving into Level 2 has been the need to move away from one's craft and the more hands-on elements of jobs that we loved. Some wondered if they would have the skills and interest to succeed with the new demands. While some embraced the chance to shift from focusing on being a team player to being a coach, many balked at the tradeoffs. For example, a lawyer talked about her trepidation in moving up in her organization, which meant giving up casework and moving on to a managerial role which she was not sure played to her strengths. She took the promotion though, and over time, she became more comfortable with the challenge of managing her department. She found that she did have a wealth of experience to draw upon, not least of which was years of learning from the good and bad behaviors of her previous supervisors. She also had to shift her way of working, designating specific time blocks in her calendar for the thinking and writing work that she loved, since so much of the week was consumed by managing her team and positioning them for success. Her conscientious efforts played off. She was rapidly recognized as a highly productive and conscientious manager and was given a high-profile assignment. Eventually, she was poached to run an international agency. None of this could have happened if she had not been willing to take the risk of taking on the next level of leadership.

Letting go is a challenge we face moving from Level 1 to Level 2. As we gain more responsibilities, we feel more pressure to deliver. We know that as leaders we can no longer do it all. We have to let go of our ability to control everything and rely more on others. We have seen managers trying to exert control by criticizing everything that crosses their desk, sending floods of midnight directives by email or simply denying travel requests or basic resources. Moreover, we ourselves have all too often fallen into the trap of micromanaging junior colleagues' outputs. In one case, a Thrive member found herself mimicking her boss's command-and-control approach. She had to intentionally shift her mindset and learn how to empower others with the space to deliver the quality work she had previously prided herself on. What she discovered was that ironically, when she stepped away from the details and consciously gave her team the "confidence to fly on their own," she gained their trust and took a big step forward as a leader.

The leaders we most admire have many tools in their toolbox when it comes to motivating people. There are carrots, which means incentives such as rewards, compensation, and recognition for a job well done. There are sticks, which come from enforcing consequences or pitting team members against each other to get their competitive juices flowing. However, the most powerful tool, particularly for social impact work, is the inspiration that people feel when you tap into their sense of purpose. We have seen time and again that people on our teams and across our organizations and networks will go way above and beyond when they believe in the mission and when they see ways that their specific role is contributing to a bigger goal that they intrinsically care about such as tackling climate change or financial inclusion.

Another key element of leadership is fostering an environment that allows our teams to thrive and advance their careers. The research undertaken by Google's Project Aristotle revealed that the most critical characteristic of high-performing teams is when team members feel they are in a safe space for shared inquiry and learning. It is painful to see others make mistakes we would not have made, and it is all too easy to react critically or just re-do the work ourselves. But when we do, we risk undermining that sense of shared purpose and trust. One of the keys Monica found was the power of inquiry to unlock ideas and solutions by asking thoughtful questions to let her team deduce their own answers. Wendy leads her team in a weekly huddle where nothing is off the table – the free flow of ideas, concerns, successes and failures helps everyone feel as though they are contributing, and their views will be welcomed. Many adjustments to their work program stem from these discussions where the team can quickly take in new information and recalibrate their work going forward. Trusting that their views will be heard and considered in this forum makes each team member feel like they have a stake in their success.

Even in the most supportive environment it can be difficult to provide negative feedback. However, without being clear headed about what worked and what didn't, there can be no improvement. Many a Thrive lunch discussion centered around how to give negative feedback to good people. What we have come to see is that it is kinder to be candid in the face of poor performance, but to do so with empathy and curiosity. Sometimes this is all it takes to identify the problem and see remarkable improvements. Yet at other times, after precise feedback and coaching has not worked, helping team members pivot to something more suitable with kindness and empathy is best. We have even seen cases where a former staff member has come back to thank the manager for their honest but constructive feedback and the nudge that led them to a more fulfilling job that was a better fit.

Ask for forgiveness, not permission

As we take on new leadership roles, it can be difficult to be comfortable asserting our own authority. In some cases, we allow others too much influence over our actions. We risk "analysis paralysis" or "death by a thousand cuts" when we become overly concerned with getting everyone in wholehearted agreement before any action is taken. We need to ask ourselves if we could move forward, even under the radar. At a Thrive lunch, one of us was struggling to decide whether or not to kick off a new project that had been hard to get her manager to review but that had general interest from various stakeholders. The group counseled her to have the courage to start mobilizing the new project calling on the mantra "ask for forgiveness, not permission." It was a powerful reminder that as leaders we have agency to do what we believe is right, even if some may do things differently. That said if we move ahead, we need to take full responsibility for our actions and be prepared to course correct, smooth things over and ask for forgiveness if the new initiative backfires or rubs someone the wrong way. Invariably, the mopping up is more than worth the cost of inaction.

Give teams the confidence to fly

While many of the challenges of Level 2 leadership have to do with building excellent teams, some of the bigger challenges relate to how our teams are positioned for success. Just like we all faced our own tiara moments personally, we need to step up as both champion and architect of our teams' success. We have spent hours over lunch, talking about how to deal with situations where our teams deserve more – more resources, more recognition, or more advocacy – and strategizing on how to get it.

There was a sensitive situation where a Thrive member wanted to promote a woman who was preparing to go on maternity leave – both because she had gone above and beyond in preparation for her extended time off as well as in recognition of the consistently reliable quality of her deliverables and behind-the-scenes nature of her work. The Thrive member strategized with another (male) partner who shared the positive impressions of this rising star and a strong desire to have her return full-time post maternity leave. They carefully crafted a promotion that recognized past achievements and provided additional awards upon return, aspiring to reward contribution and adapt to changing personal circumstances. It can be easy to overlook team members who are heads down and more focused on delivering excellent products rather than promoting their own achievements; but these are the team members that we have often found deserve our attention and recognition.

One Thrive member noted that she felt a big part of her job had become shielding her team from the unreasonable pressures emanating from her boss. She faced a situation where a toxic boss was lashing out at her and her team. The product was sub-par, but the criticism was overblown. The Thrive member first tried to address the concerns politely, deflecting the criticism and working behind the scenes to improve the product. When the hostile attitude continued – demoralizing the team and contributing to continued underperformance, she had to establish clear rules of engagement with her superiors in order to enable her team to creatively problem solve and produce better outcomes. As leaders, the buck stops with us regarding our team's wellbeing. It falls on us to advocate for our teams and their work product, and to be the first to address unreasonable expectations or criticisms of superiors, clients or other teams.

Level 3: Influence systems – Lead with clarity, conviction, empathy and agility

Level 3 is about being able to influence the rules, structures, norms and dynamics within which we function, to build a better system. To achieve this, systems-wide change involves modeling a different type of leadership style, establishing new norms of behavior and engaging others for influence. And to do so with confidence. Sustainable leadership also means it's not enough to just break through the glass ceiling but to make sure others can find new paths to success, and don't cut themselves on the shards.

New paradigms and models

Many times, we do this by role modeling the approaches we think are right. For Monica, this meant building a venture capital firm, Quona Capital, that was successful without succumbing to a "bro culture" or the ego-centric style characteristic of many well-known VCs. It meant being mindful of how incentives were structured to balance between finding and winning the best deals and learning and collaborating across the portfolio. Operationalizing this approach was arduous, as it broke with the standard practices and shifted power dynamics. At the simplest level, they renamed Monday morning all-hands gatherings (involving staff across functions and from around the globe) from investment-focused "deal rosters" to "team meetings" which kicked off with pictures of weekend activities, shout outs for above-and-beyond support and important updates. In addition, they institutionalized a new platform function designed to leverage learnings from within the deal teams across the portfolio. Taking on the difficult conversations inherent with changing the status quo required a strong awareness of her own triggers and the skills to productively discuss points of disagreement. There were many times where her frustration got the better of her. However, over time – and with the support of coaches and Thrive peers that helped her reframe the narrative – she developed more effective leadership approaches to foster a more cohesive culture that integrated different viewpoints and ways of working.

Foresight to see around corners

Another element of Level 3 leadership is being able to see the interconnections and dependencies in the systems we are trying to change, but not to let the complexity paralyze us. The ability to "see around corners" was cited by Jack Welch, the famous CEO of GE as the most essential characteristic of high-performing managers. But no one comes to see these interlinkages by themselves. We find the higher we go the more important it is to elicit the opinions of others, hear and empathize with different viewpoints and learn where others think the pressure points and opportunities are. Not only is it important to understand perspectives from our own teams, organizations and industries, but it becomes more and more important to understand how people in adjacent fields see things, because that's where opportunities, innovations and threats may come from. Such outreach has the ancillary benefit of generating new potential allies and broadening our own personal horizons.

Wendy's work to support women entrepreneurs around the world takes such a systems approach. It looks at what works and what doesn't work for women across all aspects of the entrepreneurial ecosystem. A confounding issue has been understanding the finance gap women entrepreneurs face – how big it is and what to do about it. Looking at the lack of data on the problem, she had an Aha! moment over coffee with a friend who was working on the climate crisis. Many of the same issues had been tackled to address the climate challenge. She realized that solutions that were emerging there could be applied when it came to gender financing as well. Learning more about what worked and what didn't in the climate space became a critical path to finding solutions for women.

Slow down to speed up

As we acquire data and experience to "see around corners," it can be difficult to know when to fire and when to hold our powder. After years of being asked to deliver results quickly, it can be difficult to push the pause button or leave a box unchecked. Other times, analysis paralysis can become a factor as we rise and look to effect more systemic change. We've found that picking the right time – or sometimes picking the right battle – is essential to create systems change and that rushing things can sometimes backfire. Part of this is being clear on what is important and what is essential, focusing on results and not on who gets the credit. Finding the right moment also requires both active listening and executive communication – knowing when to push back or redirect, finding real compromise to balance different perspectives and influencing decision makers to book wins. Positional power might provide agency to shape the rules in a certain way, but until one wins hearts and minds, it will not be sustainable.

With over 30 years in a large international organization, Wendy has seen her share of strategic change efforts. She has had front row seats on some of them, and other times she's been in the audience. Usually, these efforts can simply be seen as the pendulum swinging back and forth, adjusting for the realities of the market or the imperatives of growth. Other times there is a genuinely new vision that requires a shift. But what she has seen is that the chances of success of these efforts are unrelated to their merits. Peter Druker's adage that "culture eats strategy for lunch" is as true for a massive corporate restructuring effort as it is for implementing smaller systems change. The efforts that

Wendy saw creating lasting and valuable change, were those that were rooted in an understanding of the culture, norms and stakeholder incentives. The ones that did not, usually faded away no matter how much time and resources were plowed into them. Her takeaway was that if you want systems to change, you may need to go slow to go fast.

Ultimately, what is important with Level 3 leadership is not how to do it effectively, but why Level 3 leadership is needed in the first place. While we work in organizations that strive to make the world a better place, they are imperfect – as are many aspects of our society. By getting to Level 3 we can help reframe the storylines, change the rules of engagement, and give voice to the parts of the system that are broken and need to be fixed. So, getting to Level 3 also means trusting our intuition that something is not right, and to envision a better way. Whether it is toxic work environments, implicit racial or gender bias, or a lack of action on climate or other social issues, there are many fronts requiring actions big and small. To be a part of that change, we need to be able to harness all levels of our leadership skills to make a difference.

Shaping the Boundaries between Work and Life

We are at risk of losing millions of women in leadership.
—Lareina Yee, McKinsey's Chief Diversity & Inclusion Officer

It was Tuesday at 11 a.m. on a blustery March day in London. As Wendy wandered through the David Hockney exhibit at the Tate Modern museum, she couldn't shake the fear that she was going to get caught playing hooky from work. As she admired the paintings, she subconsciously ran through the excuses that she might need if she was called out. Each time she noticed her feelings of guilt, she had to pinch herself and remember why she was there. She had arrived in London that morning, for a conference the following day that both she and her Director – her boss's boss – were speaking at. As their plane had landed, her Director had asked her what her plan was for the day. She quickly jettisoned the idea of a nap and said she'd just freshen up then head right into their London office to check on some colleagues and emails. "Oh," he said, "because I was hoping to take in the new Hockney exhibit at the Tate Modern. My wife and I are huge fans and the exhibit is supposed to be great. I thought you might be interested in seeing it as well. And I always like to visit the Turner exhibit there when I'm in town."

Wendy was flabbergasted. The fact that her Director was not expecting her to rush into the office was one thing. But that he was planning to take the better part of the workday recovering from an overnight flight on a leisurely visit to a museum – and was encouraging her to do the same – was an entirely different thing. In the end, she went, and the day turned out to be refreshing, illuminating and memorable, with beautiful art and wide-ranging conversations. But the jabs of anxiety were a

43

wakeup call for her. It made her realize that her priorities were not entirely right. Her hard-working ethos was leading her astray where her boss had gotten it right. He was not afraid to prioritize moments of joy and beauty where he could, even if it meant work would need to wait sometimes. Wendy resolved to jettison the guilt and make more time for joy at work, too. Five years later, that Director, who taught Wendy so much, tragically passed away. It was a huge loss to his friends, colleagues and of course his family, but the one solace Wendy took was that she knew he had lived life to the fullest, and in doing so showed her and many others the way too.

When we have so much going on in our work and in our personal lives, the boundaries between them can get blurry. We don't want to live inflexible, compartmentalized lives that do not allow for finding joy in the in-between spaces. Yet it is also not healthy to live without boundaries, which help us to manage expectations and keep ourselves sane. We have come to see boundary-setting and flexibility as two sides of the same coin, competing but essential elements that are both required to create a harmonious balance in our lives. When and where we show up at work; when the personal and professional intersect; and how we set expectations with our colleagues – these are not just questions about our availability, but about the norms by which we treat others and expect to be treated by them.

What a difference a year makes

COVID-19 has given us a new perspective on managing the boundaries between work and home. Now that many of us have done what was once inconceivable and worked from home for more than a year, our notions of work-life balance have been transformed. Working from home has been grueling for some and liberating for others; for most it has been a little of each. One of the big realizations early on during the COVID-19 pandemic was how lucky Thrive women are to be doing knowledge-based work that can often be done effectively from home. We recognized the true hardships of the frontline workers who were on call and at risk during the pandemic and often could not be home while the kids were in virtual school. We have been grateful for the extra time we gained to talk with kids at lunch; share small victories or disappointments with our spouse in real time; or do an errand for an ailing parent during the workday. We saw some productivity gains and other productivity drains, and we missed the spontaneous and personal interactions with our colleagues that our office lives once provided.

In general, Thrive women don't want to go back to the way it was. On a Zoom call six months into the COVID-19 pandemic, nine out of ten Thrive women agreed that they did not want to go back to the intense international travel routines many of them had before. A much larger survey conducted by PwC in January 2021 indicated that nearly 60% of women were looking to return only part time to the office.[18] A McKinsey/LeanIn survey around the same time showed that 32% of women were looking to downshift or leave the workforce entirely, a number that rose to an astounding 40% for women with kids under the age of ten.[19] Encouragingly, the PwC survey also revealed that 83% of bosses said that remote work was successful in their company, opening the door for more flexible approaches going forward, and many have started experimenting with this since.

How this will change our workday in the long run is still uncertain. What is certain is that none of this will be easy. In the early 2000s, Wendy was involved in a women's group at work that decided to create a toolkit to tackle the policies and stigmas working women (and men) confronted when it came to flexwork in her organization. Some of the challenges they identified then are likely to be germane today: skeptical managers who are unwilling to approve specific arrangements even when they are permissible, worried about productivity, accountability and the effects on the intangible "office culture";

staff who are uncomfortable or unable to make the case for their request; policies that are too rigid or complex to make them worthwhile for either staff or managers. As the world of work shifts, we want to purposefully reimagine what is the right balance for us personally; and as managers, we need to think boldly about how the institutions where we work can adapt to accommodate these needs.

Dividing our time, over time

In our decade of Thrive, we saw that the pressures on our time due to work and family changed from year to year. As young go-getters we didn't have any problem putting in long hours, so taking days off to compensate for travel and late nights and weekends was the biggest need. With young children underfoot, working from home for some was an impossibility, for others a necessity to juggle competing obligations. What many of us needed most in those years was fixed, sometimes fewer, working hours to manage childcare. For some, taking one day a week off helped, while for others it was impossible to make that work. When plans to work after putting the kids to bed were regularly thwarted by a sleep-inducing bedtime story, one Thrive member scheduled a weekly "late night" in the office to get the work done. Now that the children are older, the work-from-home arrangement during the COVID-19 crisis works well for most of us, most of the time. Even people who don't have children have flexible work needs, whether it is the single woman caring for her elderly parents, the married man with an ill spouse or the burnt-out office rock star who needs a break to reset his or her mental health.

There is no one-size-fits all to flexwork. As we manage our own work/life balance and present options to our staff, we need to grapple with competing needs as we return to a more agile workplace. As managers and as professionals we have to ask: What are the essential elements to building trust and establishing accountability? How do we transmit a corporate culture and build relationships? How do younger staff learn from older staff? How do we safeguard productivity and innovation? The flexwork toolkit mentioned earlier emphasized the importance of establishing a transparent and time-bound plan for the flex-work arrangement, and clear metrics for accountability, and a very clear business case. Equally important, it advocated for having an honest discussion about the impact of flexwork on other staff members and how to evaluate the situation and unwind it if it is not working. If there was a silver bullet in the flexwork toolkit, Wendy always thought it was the recommendation that every manager proactively ask each staff member about what they need in the way of flexibility. In her experience these are always illuminating conversations that build trust and understanding and remove the stigma around the need for flexibility. Requests can be tailored to the needs of the individual and the business, making the staff more satisfied, and the working relationships even more productive.

Notwithstanding where we work, in this virtual world, the boundaries between our work and our personal time can be strained. Emails at midnight, texts at the dinner table, 6 a.m. work calls and weekend deliverables abound. It is so easy to slip into work mode without noticing it, to the detriment of our family and our own mental health. Lisa learned by trial and error how to set boundaries around her own time, and that of her team, while leading global teams living in all time zones from California to the UK and Argentina to India. On a "walk and talk," Wendy helped her see that her own habit of reading critical emails in the morning before breakfast and exercise was not only unnecessary but set her back before the day even started. Wendy's prompt inspired Lisa to carve out space in her calendar every morning and evening called the "Bella run" – a double entendre of both going for a run and taking her daughter, Bella, to and from school. In turn, she also asked team members to share their own "availability corridors." Together they agreed that it is okay to send an email when convenient to the sender, but that it is also okay for the recipient to respond when it is convenient to them. The result was that both she and her team became much more intentional about scheduling time, and respectful of the need for balance across the group.

As with many things, we hope these kinds of flexible thinking are already becoming more normal as managers are actually more likely to check in with work-at-home staff. We were delighted to see these issues highlighted in a riveting conversation between heavy hitters Christine Lagarde, the President of the European Central Bank and Ursula von der Leyen, the President of the European Commission.[20] They agreed on the importance of leadership signaling to staff that personal time should be respected, and that except for truly urgent situations, taking personal time to respond to routine work requests was not expected. As we return to the office, it will be even more important to have these regular conversations to normalize and adapt flexible work for everyone.

Bring-your-life-to-work day

In addition to the boundaries that we set for where and when we work, we carefully curate the intersections between our work and personal relationships, probably more so as we get older. It can feel perilous to bring too much of our personal selves into the office, beyond the small talk and sanctioned "bring our children to work days." However, by allowing others to see our full selves, including our vulnerabilities, we have found we can be more authentic leaders, more passionate advocates and gain more fulfillment from our work.

In the age of Zoom, it seems quaint to recall a hilarious video that was heavily circulated, of a buttoned-up man being interviewed from his home office by the BBC about policies towards North Korea. As he provides an erudite analysis of the geopolitical situation, his toddler skips into the room, followed by an infant in a baby walker. While he tries to remain stoic, eventually the harried mother slides in, grasping at the children to pull them out of the camera view. At the time, the scene encapsulated so much of what we felt as working mothers, with so much of our lives hidden behind a wall, always in jeopardy of becoming embarrassingly visible. That it was a man having the experience made it all the more cathartic to watch.

With COVID-19, we have all become "BBC man," and this in the long run may become one of the most significant shifts for the way we work.[21] As Zoom became the new normal, we have seen a CEO revealing that below his collared shirt and desk, he is in shorts and bare feet; a bank CEO giving instructions to her daughter on how to bake a birthday cake for her husband; an Oscar-winning producer fretting about her anxious dog lingering in the camera frame; and a foundation president's basement strewn with video game consoles and darts. These peeks behind the curtain have given us insights, helped us become more empathetic and created confidence as we see that both our role models and our peers are "just like us" and they are not embarrassed to show it.

We also have found that greater openness can work for us. When Monica was considering a partner for her venture fund, she invited him to dinner at her house, wanting the prospective partner to understand the full person that he would be partnering with. That meant not just dinner in a sanitized environment, but meeting the spouse and kids, seeing their art on the walls, the husband's hobbies displayed on shelves, and the neighborhood they had chosen to settle in. That may be an uncomfortable prospect for some of us, but it has allowed her to be a more authentic partner and leader with her team as a result. What we are learning is that seeing – and showing – what can sometimes be the messy side of our personal lives, can actually help us build more trusting and effective relationships at work.

It takes two to tango

Although we are convinced that we need a more nuanced approach to setting boundaries that allows for flexibility, we also recognize that if only working women are removing screens and pulling down walls, it may well backfire. Notwithstanding the peek inside that COVID-19 has given us, there are still many who are uncomfortable when work gets too personal. For every mother who keeps the screens up, there is a father doing the same, who possibly feels even more pressure to keep that part of their lives hidden. People without children can also feel uncomfortable or judged when personal obligations intersect with work, whether it be other caregiving responsibilities or other pursuits. For working mothers to feel comfortable bringing their whole self to work, others need to feel comfortable doing the same. As leaders, we can do more to encourage that in our workplace.

Finding ways to invite others to share aspects of their personal lives is key. One woman insists that when she is introduced as a speaker at an event, her biography includes mention of her children and asks that other speakers also share information about their family. There is also clear evidence that asking business leaders who are also fathers of daughters to talk about their aspirations for their daughters, actually changes their behavior at work.[22] They become more empathetic to women employees, better allies in promoting and supporting women, and role model positive behaviors for other men. Alexis Ohanian, the co-founder of Reddit who may be better known as Serena Williams' husband, has been an amazing and visible advocate on this topic. He sees this starting with paternity leave, which is so important at the personal level to build the bond between father and child, while also making the parental roles at home and at work more equitable (as has been the case in Iceland).[23] For society as a whole, as more men proudly and visibly take substantial paternity leave, other men will be inspired to be more open about that aspect of their personal lives, ultimately making it a new normal and reducing the stigma for working mothers.

Keeping women at the table

As we navigate the day-to-day questions around where to draw lines between work and our personal lives, women often consider the merits not just of flexwork, but of opting out of the workforce altogether. In a McKinsey/Lean In study from the fall of 2020, one in four women said they were thinking of leaving the workforce.[24] At the same time, during the COVID-19 pandemic the annual rate of high-propensity start-ups in the US doubled as people leave the workforce (voluntarily or not) and seek a different path.

Many of us have considered stepping away from full-time work for greater balance and fulfillment that work was not providing. We admire (and are sometimes a bit envious of) friends who have made these choices, especially as many have found ways to have a deep and lasting impact on their families and communities in their new roles. But we also regret the loss of those voices around the table at work and wonder if there are not ways to allow women who want to pursue careers better flexibility to do both. Most of our friends who have left the workforce, did so not because they want to spend their days in carpools and yoga pants, or suddenly had an epiphany that a woman's place is in the home. The choice to walk away from a career that they have invested in and often are passionate about was difficult. Nevertheless, they make a calculated decision that they can contribute more and have a more fulfilling life not working full time or in a career-track job. Many have also made a rational economic calculation: since many women earn less than their male partners, the impact on the family budget is less severe.

The truth is that women who can afford to walk away or downshift often find the scales heavily weighted against remaining on the professional track. Not only are there myriad subtle and sometimes overt cultural and personal reminders of the value of mothers being at home, but opportunities are growing for them to make contributions in their communities, through part-time work or the gig economy on more flexible terms. When women are not promoted, shifted to "mommy-track" jobs or not given opportunities to shine, the balance shifts more towards opting out. This seems to be exacerbated as we get older and positions become more competitive, which is often also when bias and microaggressions come into play, further tipping the balance away from work.

When women walk away from the workplace, it is mostly bad for the workplace. Not only are employers limiting their access to an enormous pool of talent, they are losing a powerful model of managerial skills that are reinforced in parenting: empowering self-reliance, adapting with growth, choosing battles. Many of our friends and colleagues have chosen to take time off when their children are young but are interested in restarting their careers as the children grow. As both employees and employers, we can be much more thoughtful about how we structure those transitions to maintain open connections, skills and information to smooth the possibility for re-entry.

Lisa spent many sleepless nights on maternity leave wondering how she was going to be able to manage the demands of being a new mother with the often-relentless travel required by consultants. As luck would have it, when she was returning from maternity leave – an important and vulnerable time for any woman – she heard that a leader who had championed her work earlier in her career was looking for a strategy lead for the company's corporate citizenship team. The focus would be on shaping sustainability approaches for her own company, rather than consulting on the same with external clients. Lisa jumped at the serendipitous offer for two reasons. Here was a unique chance to "walk the talk" on a topic she cared about, aligning her personal passion to her day job. Equally critical at that time in her life, the new role gave her the ability to frequently work from home. Among the many other benefits, she was able to work remotely for many summers in her husband's hometown in Spain so her daughter could grow up immersed in her Spanish family, culture and language.

For those who care about making sure women leaders are at the table (as we certainly do), we need to strengthen the positives associated with work, which includes enabling greater balance between work and personal lives. With COVID-19, the balance has shifted and we see more ways that work and home life can co-exist. There is greater openness to working from home in most organizations. There is also more flexibility in terms of physical versus virtual presence with the rapid adoption of zoom and other digital communication technologies. There is greater understanding of what goes on behind the curtain in the care economy. Leaders like Jacinda Ardern, the acclaimed Prime Minister of New Zealand, who brought her newborn baby to her speech at the UN General Assembly, show that women can deliver and manage the various aspects of their lives if they have the options.[25] By finding new ways to accommodate their needs, we will stem the exodus and keep more women at the table, benefiting us all.

Building and Nurturing
Families that Thrive

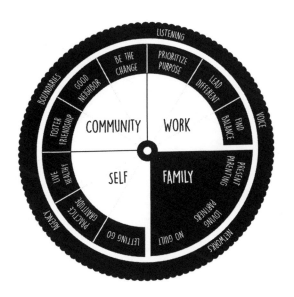

No matter what is happening at work, we are first and foremost mothers, spouses and daughters. The highs and lows of family life can make even the biggest victories and most dramatic failures at work pale in comparison. If a kid is struggling at school, it weighs heavily on us while even modest victories can make our hearts sing. If a spouse or parent is struggling, it is our struggle too. One of the fundamental desires that drives our Thrive conversations is to find ways to make sure our families thrive as they grow and change. The tensions between our work life and our family life are real, and we ask a lot of ourselves: How can we be fully present with our children and spouses, and truly listen to them, when there are so many distractions? How do we stay on the same page with our partners throughout the roller coaster of family life and as our relationships evolve? And (over and over again!), how do we balance our energy between our work and our family without being overwhelmed by guilt?

Being Present, Supportive Parents

Encourage and support our kids, as children are apt to live up to what you believe of them.
—Lady Bird Johnson

One evening, Lisa came home from work to her fourth-floor apartment, deep in thought about a recent conflict at work. As she put her things away, she absentmindedly greeted her daughter, Bella. After several unsuccessful attempts by Bella to draw Lisa into conversation, Bella asked chirpily, "Mom, is it okay if I jump out the window?" Without missing a beat, Lisa murmured, "Yes, sure." When she looked up to see her daughter's eyebrows raised high, they both burst out laughing. Her daughter knew all too well how distracted Lisa could get and had finally found a funny way to needle her about her frustrating habit. Lisa and her family often laugh about that moment. It has become a symbol for them of the need to give each other their full attention and really listen.

Navigating with a compass, but no map

The Thrive women's children range from two to eighteen years old, but most are now pre-teens or teenagers. Among the authors, Wendy has three children, Monica has two and Lisa has one. Plus two dogs who often seem like additional boisterous kids in the house. Most of us have made it through the infant and toddler years, elementary school, and find ourselves the mothers of sometimes sweet, sometimes surly teenagers. When we look ahead, we see their impending departure for college and imminent launch into adulthood and wonder if we're doing all we can to prepare them well. While we can look back and see some things that worked and others not so much, we are still muddling through.

We want what all parents want. We want our kids to live a great life and reach their full potential. We want them to love and be loved, to connect with friends and their community and to be curious and inspired by the world around them. We want them to be motivated to learn, grow, and engage so that they can follow their own passions and be the agents of their own destiny.

Our children are incredibly lucky to be growing up with all of the advantages, support, love, education, and outlets that anyone could hope for. Yet they are growing up at a time full of paradoxes. On the one hand, they live in a world of technological and human progress and prosperity that would have been unfathomable to their great-grandparents.[26] On the other hand, they are growing up in a world with many anxieties, far beyond the standard-fare growing pains and social awkwardness we faced as children. Climate change, school shootings, political turmoil, pandemics, and the vagaries of social media just top the list. There are no good roadmaps, no simple good and bad guys, no easy solutions to these challenges. Nor are there simple answers for how we help our children navigate them.

At our Thrive lunches the underlying questions have been consistent: How can we help our kids preserve the joy and hope of childhood into adulthood? How can we help them build the grit and emotional resilience they need to face these challenges life will throw at them? When they were under eight or so, in many ways the conversations were simpler. We needed hacks to physically make it through the grueling early days (and nights) of motherhood. We needed tips on schools, camps, and childcare. We looked for advice to soothe sibling rivalries and hurt feelings. Looking back, it seems we had it in our power to "fix" many of the challenges our little ones had. As they grow older, we are losing the ability to "fix" everything that comes up. The days when a crying baby could be soothed by her mother's milk, a toddler could be distracted by a chocolate chip cookie, or a time-out could solve a sibling squabble are long gone. Just as we had to learn to let go to get to Level 2 leadership at work, we are learning how to let go with our children, while keeping guardrails in place to help them succeed.

Over the decade that we have been talking, our children have grown up considerably. Over that same time, their struggles have gotten more complex. But surprisingly we have noticed that our best parenting moments have come when we have followed a handful of time-tested principles, some voiced by our own parents or grandparents. More consequentially, our failures have usually come when we have not followed those principles. The things we keep coming back to have nothing to do with being a tiger mom or helicopter parent. They may be the opposite of those now popular parenting stereotypes. Instead, they include being more present with our children, listening more intently to what they are truly saying, encouraging them to have a growth mindset, and giving them the space to figure things out for themselves.

The joy of slowing down and being in the moment

When we are rushing around, juggling work and family in our pre-COVID-19 frenzy, we find that it's easy to miss important moments. There is the obvious ignominy of missing a ballet recital or holiday pageants. At Thrive lunches we've also shared stories of catching ourselves sorting and cleaning up Lego instead of just sitting and enjoying building a Lego castle with our toddler. Sometimes, it is just a matter of having the presence of mind to slow down and quiet the voices in our head, so that we can be fully there for our children. Over time we've come upon various techniques to center ourselves and be more present, and learned how important it is to our kids, our spouses and colleagues when we do so.

Monica has a vivid memory of a fall evening in DC. The sun was setting over the park behind her house and she could feel a chill in the air. Overlooking the cold and her tired body, she joined in on the nightly football toss her son loved. The brisk movement and her son's laughter warmed her soul, even as her fingers stiffened. Reflecting on that moment or the times she's spent kicking the soccer ball around with her daughter, she sees these precious moments being active together as gifts. The more of them she's had with her twins the more they've built on each other and changed the tone of how they related to each other. Looking back, she can see how those fun times together, when she was fully present, have helped to shift their conversations and made even difficult ones easier. As working moms, we are constantly searching for those moments and recognize even when they are fleeting, they can be powerful.

Whether it is presence of mind or physical presence, often it just takes a little time to make a difference. But sometimes it takes more. When our kids really need us, sometimes the pause needs to be longer and the focus more sustained. When that happens, we need to be there for our kids with grace and have the presence of mind to respond to what's happening in the moment. One of Wendy's daughters was struggling with middle school as the world ground to a halt with COVID-19. Beforehand, always busy with travel and work, Wendy had tried to figure out what was happening, often in snippets on calls while traveling and when they were both home; tired from work and school. When Wendy's work became fully virtual and the whole family was at home 24/7, Wendy realized what a gift it was to be there day-in and day-out to check in, observe and help get things back on track. The time we spent at home during the pandemic has in many ways been a huge privilege for the Thrive women. It has given us more time to be present with our children just as they are drifting towards their own paths. It has also made us realize that the "new normal" for working parents needs to allow for more flexibility to work from home and be present for even those small moments that matter.

Listening with nothing on our mind

Often as working parents, we listen with something on our mind. As a kid tells us about his latest book report we're wondering: What time do we have to leave for school to get to work on time? How can I make dinner and also respond to that email that just came in? How can I solve this scheduling problem? How can I get them to see things my way? We've learned the hard way that when we listen to them with nothing on our mind, we can really hear and respond to our kids. If we stop running through the lengthy "to do" list lurking in our mind and really listen deeply, our kids will feel our presence. They know the difference instantly and instinctively. Not only will they open up more easily, but they will get to their point more quickly than if we're not paying attention.

We have also come to realize that listening intently with a quiet mind can also mute the natural tendency of parents to jump in with ill-conceived attempts to solve their child's stated problem. Particularly with teenagers and pre-teens, if kids are sharing something with their parents it may be to just get it off their chest. If this is the case, the moment a parent starts rattling off what they would do, it can have a chilling effect on the conversation. We've all had the experience of being in what we feel is a good conversation, only to have the kid turn on a dime mid conversation and clam up inexplicably.

The alternative we've learned is to get curious about what's being said. Instead of moving into "I can solve this for you" mode, we find it can be better first to ask about the ground rules, i.e., "Do you want some help thinking through this or do you just want to tell me this?" When we have confirmation that our daughter has shared all that she wanted to, the door is open to either share a story of how we handled something similar when we were young or to ask an open-ended question that could prompt our kids to give us some ideas about how they would like to handle the situation.

All the women in Thrive have stories about how they were not proud of an angry reaction they had to their child when they had just "lost it." We strive to find ways to be "calm parents," to manage our own anger response, finding ways to self-regulate and to bring humor to diffuse tense moments and not let ourselves be triggered. Yet we have empathetically compared – and laughed over – stories of when we did not show up as our best selves. We have shared resources that helped each other course correct, like child development books that detail "age appropriate" responses, explore common parental triggers and provided frameworks and tools we could try out.[27] These have helped us find our own paths to better parenting.

With the benefit of hindsight, we've seen how at each age and stage, there are different ways to connect with our kids that meet them where they are. When they are babies, it's easy enough to just sit down on the floor, forget about work, and jump into whatever is going on, whether it's rolling a ball around or building a fort. In the teenage years it can sometimes be harder to find the entry points. A Thrive member shared that the beauty of the digital age is that if all lines of communication with your teenager are under duress, "you can always text." This is perhaps the one advantage of the phone seeming like an appendage to a teen.

Another handy place for communication is the car. There's something universal and powerful about opening up with someone when we're side by side facing the same direction and in motion. Wendy remembers listening in astonishment to the conversations her daughter Naoma and her friends would have in the carpool to and from ballet. They provided such insights to the world that her daughter was in and how she saw herself in it. When it was just the two of them driving, Naoma would also be more likely to open up about things that she normally kept to herself, giving Wendy glimmers of the things that were exciting or worrying her. On long trips they could spend hours discussing elaborate narratives Naoma was writing in her spare time, illuminating a growing perspective on the world around her. Facing the same direction provides a natural buffer or a moment of pause to recompose before an automatic reaction is triggered by something a kid says or does. There's a sense of flow and going in the same direction which can be a great trigger for closeness and sharing. We've seen this in cars, just like on our "walk and talks." We've come to relish our time taking kids to and from school for this very reason.

Unlocking the growth mindset

Instilling competence and confidence in our kids is important. We know tiger moms who demand their children reach Ivy League school standards and dads that scream from the sidelines like their seven-year-old is playing in the World Cup. At the other extreme, we have seen the "everyone's a winner" trophies and parents who praise their children indiscriminately. Those extremes have not worked for us and we often talk about what does.

When Wendy was nursing her son, she read a book that greatly influenced her called *The Childhood Roots of Adult Happiness*[28] which emphasized the importance of helping children find mastery doing things they loved. It could be anything, large or small but it had to be theirs. Pushing them to achieve excellence where their heart was not in it would not make them happy, but nor would letting them languish without a passion. She saw this clearly play out with her son, Tibor. He had played soccer and ultimate frisbee in elementary school, but he never truly loved either sport. While she and her husband encouraged him to continue, his heart was not in it. In middle school, he enjoyed skateboarding with a group of friends, but felt he was missing out without an organized sport or a team. When he was entering High School, his father signed him up for a crew camp, almost on a lark. It was a match made in heaven. Tibor hardly knew what the sport was when he got on the water for the first time, but from the start, he loved and excelled at it. The sport and the team have been the defining element of his high school experience, giving him the confidence and discipline to take on challenges in many other parts of his life.

We cannot have mastery without a growth mindset, the belief that we can learn and grow through curiosity, dedication and effort. In her book *Grit*, Angela Duckworth shares how she consciously tries to build the growth mindset in herself and her family.[29] At the start of every school year she asks each member of her family to pick out something they want to learn. It can be anything – from learning to cook a crepe from scratch to counting to a thousand in Chinese. She explains that it's the act of starting as a beginner and moving up in mastery – with all the failures and discomforts along the way – that builds grit and the growth mindset.

During the COVID-19 pandemic, we all had to learn new things. Just as COVID-19 set in, Lisa's family moved to South Florida in the height of summer heat and humidity. The hot weather was quite a shock to the system for Lisa's daughter, but she cleverly turned it around when she heard a neighbor lamenting how cold she felt watching her kid's ice hockey practice. Bella loved the idea of being on the ice and in no time was out on the rink learning how to play. Her willingness to tackle a tough new sport as a novice skater was impressive. As she made beginner loops around the rink, she could see the more seasoned players zipping around backwards at high speed and was undaunted – growth mindset in action. It requires chutzpah and also a self-belief that we'll be able to learn something new, even if it is clearly going to be a challenge.

What the growth mindset teaches us is that the key to praise is to bring attention to the process: "I can see how hard you pushed yourself in the game." or "I love how much attention you gave to the shading of the face in this picture." By putting the emphasis and praise on the act or the struggle versus the win or the grade, we boost kids' pride in their effort and remove the tension that we must win the game or get an "A": over-emphasis on the win can have the opposite effect by raising performance anxiety. The more we encourage our kids to think for themselves and remind them they have the capacity and the creativity to solve their own problems, the more we can help kids to build these critical life skills.

Paradox of expectations

While we encourage our children to build a growth mindset, we realize there is a fine line between setting aspirations that can motivate us and setting expectations that leave us feeling anxious and unable to move forward. How do we help our kids do the former knowing full well that there will be perceived failures as life happens? How do we help our kids embrace life's twists and turns and have the confidence to open more doors than they shut? How do we help our kids be comfortable setting bold goals while being willing to allow those goals to evolve over time? To have the resilience to pick themselves up off the mat whenever they fall down?

When Lisa was a few weeks from giving birth, she remembers being surprised by the parenting advice of a friend with two teens. He encouraged the mother-to-be to "lower her expectations," positing that this was the key to happiness. If you don't expect perfection and bliss from the first minute you lay eyes on your newborn, you will not be disappointed the tenth night in a row with no sleep.

There is a well-known equation that brings this to life: *"happiness equals reality minus expectations."* As we guide our children, both sides of this equation are essential. On the one hand we want them to understand that they have the power to do their best and create conditions to thrive. Lisa's daughter waged a campaign to get a puppy that included years of cajoling and powerpoint presentations that eventually succeeded when the family moved from apartments to a home with a backyard during COVID-19. Bringing home the puppy, Lisa was sure to point out to her daughter that this is what it feels like when you hold onto a dream and work hard to make sure it comes true in one form or another. On the other hand, while we want our children to pursue their dreams, we don't want them to be unhappy if they fall short or the goalposts change.

With seven kids between us, we wonder if there may be different ways to set expectations that produce different results – particularly when it comes to role modeling for our kids. We've heard how the "smartest kid in the room" may be so paralyzed by success as to not want to try hard on a test or try something new for fear of failure since the bar is set so high. We've read about women who decide in high school or college to take themselves out of the running for a high-powered career for fear of how their life might unfold. We've seen friends with elaborate birthing plans be disappointed when their experience inevitably went a different way.

Recently, Wendy's colleague asked her what gave her the confidence to champion a bold initiative that seemed to many to be out of reach at the time. Reflecting on this, Wendy realized that in formulating the "moonshot" idea, two factors were essential: first was having the vision and conviction to bring along others and persevere in pursuit of the goal. The second was a willingness to allow the process, or even the goalposts, to shift. She recognized that failure, if it came to that, was an option and would be a learning experience, but not a catastrophe. While the first factor was essential to articulate and achieve the goal, Wendy's mental health and resilience were much more dependent on the second factor.

We look to instill such ambition and persistence in our kids and to reward them for it, but also make sure they don't hold on so strongly to their (or our) expectations that anything other than perfection will leave them disappointed.

Choices with guardrails

One of the questions that Thrive women struggle with is how best to establish consequences. Kids need us to be there, like a swimming pool wall they can launch off of and come back to.[30] Teens need us to give them the space to make their own mistakes and to take responsibility for their own behavior. The question is where's the best point to remove the support? And what kind of guardrails should be there just in case?

There's a turning point when kids take responsibility for their own behavior as they have internalized it. A few months before she turned thirteen, one Thrive member's daughter started pushing back mightily when it was time to enforce the nightly 9 p.m. rule of picking up electronics and placing them in the family room. She said it made her feel like her parents didn't trust her and that she had no freedom to have this nightly nag. After some difficult nights, she asked to bring them out herself without any reminder. Once the nightly request to hand over the goods episodes stopped, the electronics magically appeared. Her sense of personal responsibility kicked in, and a sense of peace replaced the nightly tension.

We have learned how important it is to provide freedom for kids to choose within boundaries. What vegetable would you like to eat? Carrots or broccoli? What would you like to do outside this afternoon? Go for a walk or a bike ride? Do you want to clean your room before or after soccer? By setting a clear expectation and then giving kids the choice to pick however they can satisfy that expectation, parents are able to set some ground rules, norms and values; and kids are able to exercise their agency which allows them to internalize rules and make them their own.

As we've reflected on all of the hard-won lessons we've learned as parents, we have often noted how frequently the challenges we face with our children are similar to those we face with colleagues at work, our spouses and others. It follows then, that many of the solutions have similar roots: listening; being present; setting boundaries and getting curious. Head-to-head negotiation with a teenager – or a toddler for that matter – is excellent preparation for the toughest contract negotiations at work or delicate discussions with a husband. Likewise, when we learn to slow down and be present with our children, we can use that skill set with our clients, team members or aging parents. Often framed as competing or contradictory skill sets, we believe motherhood (and fatherhood) can give us superpowers at work if we just connect the dots.

Aligning our North Stars as Partners

Most of us will have multiple marriages, some of us with the same person.
—Esther Perel

Monica had been carefully curating her dating checklist for years, honing it to perfection during weekly brunches with three of her girlfriends. Smart and ambitious? Check. Same religion? Check. Gets along with the parents? Check. Fit and outdoorsy? Check. But here she was, having just broken off her engagement with a guy she thought had checked off all the boxes, wondering what to do about the list that somehow had failed her. Willing herself to jump back into the dating game, she and her friend David agreed to throw a "one-hit wonder" party, where each guest had to bring a song from a band with only one hit, and a single friend. Well into the evening, she noticed Wendy (who was grandfathered in as a married friend) talking to someone she didn't recognize. The album *Love Stinks* hung inauspiciously from his neck. Her hopes for the evening were fading, so there was nothing to lose by approaching them. He was engaging and funny, but almost immediately her checklist was on high alert. He bikes to work! Check! Oh, on a motorcycle? (uncheck). He loves to travel! Check! But not to developing countries? (uncheck). He's passionate about food! Check! But he does not eat vegetables?! (uncheck!). While she enjoyed talking to him, she could see clearly that he didn't check the boxes. So when she agreed to join him and their mutual friend at dinner later that week, she had no expectations. Her checklist had spoken.

And yet the more Monica got to know Jordan, the more she appreciated his curiosity about the world, ability to make his friends laugh, engage people from different backgrounds, and his passion for life. A few weeks later, Wendy could hear the excitement in her voice when she talked about the fun they were having and his *joie de vivre*. So it came as a surprise when just a few minutes later in the conversation, Monica said abruptly, "I think I should just break up with him now. It's obvious it will never work. He. Doesn't. Eat. Vegetables.... And I'm a vegetarian!" Wendy burst out laughing. The checklist had run amok. It was clearly not serving its purpose anymore. The list had grown so long and bizarrely specific as Monica's dating years progressed, that it had become untenable. It took a few dates to discover what lay beneath the surface with Jordan – his genuine caring about people, his curiosity about the world, his playful joy. Soon enough, Monica acknowledged that it was the checklist that wasn't fitting Jordan, not the other way around. She buried the checklist, married Jordan and twenty years plus two kids later, cannot imagine a more fitting life partner.

Warren Buffett, the investment guru and "Sage of Omaha," stated that "the most important career decision you'll ever make is who you marry."[31] We couldn't agree more. Of the 20 or so women who have participated in Thrive over the years, all were married and only one has gotten divorced. Yet, in that moment, staring at our checklist, we didn't necessarily know which characteristics were critical and which were superfluous. We still don't know, but with a couple of decades of hindsight, we can start to see with greater clarity what works and what doesn't when we partner for life.

Sharing the lead

It is the nature of the Thrive group that all of the members work long hours and many travel extensively around the world. Some are the main breadwinners in their families, while others share that responsibility with their husbands. They are also actively involved with their families and their communities, but they can't do it alone. Their spouses are their partners and finding the special formula that makes that partnership work is a constant and evolving labor of love. Old formulas of parenting no longer apply, but new ones are still evolving. We feel that we are often making it up as we go along. The fact that our husbands are willing to work with us to find that balance and accept that we both will need to make sacrifices, is probably the secret sauce that makes it all work.

Anne Marie Slaughter wrote a seminal article questioning whether women could have it all when she left her high-powered job at the US State Department in DC to focus on her family that had remained in Princeton. The ensuing debates shone a spotlight on her own career choices and on the role her husband, Andrew Moravcsik, had played as the primary parent of their children during the years she was in DC. Moravcsik eventually penned his own article in *The Atlantic*[35] about the outdated ways we think about motherhood and fatherhood, and how we need a new concept for the parent that takes the lead at home that is gender neutral. He coined the phrase "lead parent" for this role that has helped us put a word to the evolving reality of many of us.

Indeed, many men, like some of our husbands, have taken on a much greater share of the household burden than in times past. Yet in spite of these changes, old habits die hard. Professional women working in dual income households still bear about 50% more of the work on the home front. Research by Lean In and Survey Monkey during the COVID-19 crisis showed how the pandemic exacerbated this situation. It noted that "Women who work full-time and have partners and children are more than twice as likely as men in the same situation to feel that they have more to do than they can possibly handle (31% vs. 13%)."[33] On average, they spent 40 hours on childcare (7 hours more than their men), 10 hours caring for elderly or sick relatives (twice what men spent), and 7 more hours than men on housework.

Passing the baton

The "Lead Parent" concept resonates with us because it allows us to think about the elements of parenting without recourse to old gender stereotypes. As we try to balance and calibrate how we share the load with our partners, we have found that focusing on how mothers and fathers can both truly lead, maybe in different ways and at different times, has been essential. This requires a continual and intentional process of dialogue and planning to ensure that evolving career and family needs are being attended to in a way that balances shifting demands of each spouse.

When Monica first met Jordan, she was new in her job and still proving herself. Jordan – a few years her senior and more established in his career, made more money and had more job security. But Jordan had professional ambitions outside his formal job that were more creative and entrepreneurial in nature. Work for him had been more a way to pay the bills than to fulfill a passion. Monica on the other hand was passionate about her work and driven to help build an industry that she believed could change the face of poverty around the world. By the time Monica had their twins, she had been offered a compelling opportunity to manage a venture fund set up with Accion's unprecedented windfall from the sale of a microfinance institution in Mexico, Compartamos, that Monica had helped get to scale. Around the same time, Jordan's industry imploded with the global financial crisis, and he found himself thinking about what he wanted next. The realities of their respective careers resulted in Jordan taking on a bigger role at home while Monica began the juggling act. The combination of the life-altering impact of having one's first child (let alone two at once!), flipping the breadwinner roles and adjusting career expectations all simultaneously forced a recalibration. For Jordan, becoming lead parent was not trivial, given Monica's work and travel schedule. It meant having to assume lead responsibility for school activities and extracurriculars, putting on hold different hobbies that he had pursued over the years, and tighter schedules and budgets.

Quieting the urge to step in

Moms usually take on the "lead parent" role immediately after birth, so it can require an intentional recalibration to shift onto more equal footing. What we have found is that when dads take greater parental leadership, the hardest thing for moms is to resist the tendency to step in or remind our spouses to do it our way. Recent research has shown that even when men are stepping up to pitch in and divide work, the share of mental burden and worry is not usually evenly distributed. The "cognitive labor" involved in household management still falls disproportionately on mothers, whether they are working or not.[34] That is, our husbands may take the kids to the soccer game, but coordinating their schedules, finding the soccer cleats, managing the snacks, checking the weather and washing the clothes will more often fall to Mom. In other words, we are often still keeping control over what happens, even if who is doing it is changing.

At first, Monica tried to actively support Jordan with parenting. She would reach out to parents and organize play dates. She would volunteer for school committees. She would plan menus on Sunday and shop for the week (in the process becoming a proselytizer of plantoeat.com) and set the nightly dinner plan. All of these were at a fraction of the time Jordan spent, and it ended up becoming a source of frustration rather than support. Unspoken expectations and corresponding disappointments got buried in favor of just getting through the day. It is *not* that Jordan asked or even expected her to take on an additional burden at home: it was a subtle, subconscious narrative she had internalized around what it meant to "be a good mom." Even decisions on meal prep became a topic to navigate – harmonizing Monica's ideal of home cooked, healthy meals that had been a mainstay of her upbringing versus Jordan's "good enough" approach that defaulted to simpler solutions. But were vegetables really a topic worth quibbling over?

Aligning expectations and loosening "control" allowed Monica to *connect* more with her husband and deepen their relationship beyond the functional (splitting chores, raising kids, earning money). They learned more about each other's style (e.g., sandwiches require less prep time and clean up!) and found ways to build on each other (Jordan's mastery of whipping cream became handy in Monica's broccoli soufflé). By letting go of the urge to manage and giving her spouse some room to develop his own approach, parenting became a partnership *and* a pleasure. They became more of a sounding board for each other to navigate difficult situations and a source of emotional support. Monica credits Jordan not only with shaping their kids' upbringing but with her growth as a leader. As Esther Perel put it: "We [partners] co-create each other. Relationships are feedback loops."[36] And just like our careers – where many women have "intervals" where they pull back to accommodate the realities of balancing work and home[37] – maintaining equilibrium with our spouses requires continual recalibration.

For many of us, work travel left our husbands with primary care responsibility for significant amounts of time – in some cases up to half the year. As with many aspects of our lives, the pandemic laid bare the gymnastics required to complete even basic tasks, creating more empathy for what it takes just to get through the day. Working from home, we noticed and appreciated even more all the small things required to get the kids healthily fed, engaged in school, participating in extracurriculars, and cared for emotionally. It made it clear why our families were hungry for our attention and engagement when we arrived home – even when we arrived from work drained. COVID-19 has enabled us to find greater harmony, learning to create rituals to formally put work away (leaving the phone at the door), give each other a break, and make space to shift mindsets (from the job to home) and be fully present.

Focusing on each other

Finding ways to refuel and reconnect with our spouses was a topic of many a Thrive lunch. It is so easy to fall into the role of co-project managers with soccer games to get to, homework to be done, and dishwashers to be fixed. Finding the time and the energy to simply enjoy being with our spouses can often be the last thing on our to-do list. Date nights were a popular strategy – especially fixing a recurring calendar item carved out for our spouses. Others found smaller, more frequent rituals just as important – like having dinner alone with one's spouse versus as a family, taking a walk or doing a crossword puzzle together. The reward was finding time for each other to reconnect and building the reserves of love and purpose that they could tap during challenging times.

John Gottman's treatise The Seven Principles for Making Marriage Work, argues convincingly that successful marriages rest on simple strategies – like sharing fondness and admiration with each other, turning towards each other with big and little concerns, and finding ways to create shared meaning.[38] He finds that marriages meet their demise when they are overcome by what he calls the four horsemen: criticism, contempt, defensiveness and stonewalling. In marriages like ours, with children and when both parents work or take non-traditional parenting roles, there are unique stressors that were the topic of many a Thrive lunch.

With three kids and busy lives, Wendy and Max had to work to find the time to really connect with one another. While they got great joy from getting together regularly with friends (until COVID-19), they had a harder time carving out time with each other. Even when they did, date nights usually started with an hour or two reviewing calendars and catching up on the checklist. They found that while date nights would do in a pinch, really getting away for a day or two had a much bigger impact. Finding an opportunity to tag along on a spouse's business trip or have an older cousin come to watch the kids for a weekend getaway, has made it fun for the kids and parents. It has been in these moments when the kids were safe in other peoples' hands, where they can turn off the checklist, enjoy a laugh with each other and reconnect with what made them fall in love with each other in the first place. No matter how hard it is to find the time or make the time for those moments, it is always worth it in the end.

Gratitude and communicating the unspoken

More than one Thrive woman has noticed with an embarrassed laugh that their initial "wheel" drawing made no mention of their husband. As women have found for centuries, it often happens that we take for granted our spouses and do not give them the gratitude that they deserve. Many Thrive women cultivate an intentional practice of expressing gratitude through journals or meditation. Taking time to appreciate our spouses has become part of that practice. Sometimes it is just a matter of taking more explicit note for even small things that their spouse might do in the course of an ordinary day – like making a cup of coffee, schlepping the kids to a rainy soccer game or fixing a jammed window. Other times it can be a more existential point of thanks. Sometimes we can work together to cultivate gratitude for one another.

During the COVID-19 pandemic, after moving to Florida where it was possible to be outside year-round and for kids to be at school in person, Lisa and Álvaro started taking nightly gratitude walks around their new neighborhood thanking their lucky stars to have found a way to navigate through such a difficult time in the best way they could for their family. Back in DC, Monica bought Jordan a griddle – not just as a small thank you for making breakfast but in recognition of how pancake brunches, more than salads at dinner, became family comfort food and their family's "little ant stories" – how Jordan describes the chatter at a picnic that fills the space – create shared meaning as much as family mission statements (like Bruce Feiler described in *The Secrets of Happy Families* toolkit).[39]

There are bigger moments for gratitude as well. For their wedding, Lisa and her husband, Álvaro, developed their own set of "Ten Loving Couple Commandments" to serve as their vows. They chose to create a new tradition to bridge their upbringings, cultures, and faiths between the US and Spain, Catholicism and Judaism. They loved finding and celebrating the fundamental values that they shared and wanted to uphold through their union, and committing to those vows in front of friends and family in four cities and two countries as part of their "World Wide Wedding Tour."

When their daughter, Bella, was born, they updated the vows to be their "Loving Family Commandments" to include her. And at their ten-year wedding anniversary, celebrated at Monica's house, they asked Bella to join in the ceremony and help them update the vows to include her perspective. She asked them to add "play" to the original vow of "live life without fear" so it would read "play and live without fear." This addition was a beautiful reminder to push ourselves to look at life from different perspectives. From the playground, to the dining room, to the Boardroom. By creating their own living commandments that could evolve as their family grew, the couple was able to create their own foundation with the best of their upbringing and beliefs into their family unit.

Investing in these rituals and gestures is well worth the investment of time and energy. Thrive women share Esther Perel's view that "the quality of our life ultimately depends on the quality of our relationships."

Working Moms Without Guilt

Motherhood is about being a model, not a martyr: Children will only let themselves live as fully as we [moms] do.
—Glennon Doyle

Wendy was about to pay for the panini and coffee that would get her through the four-hour train ride from Amsterdam to the meeting in London when her phone rang. On the other end she heard the panicked voice of her husband. Dropping everything she searched out a quiet space amid the din of the train station as she tried to ignore all the alarms going off in her head. "Don't worry, everything is okay," her husband said, the words and his strained tone signaling exactly the opposite. "It's just that I don't know what to do. I think I need to go to the store to buy tampons or pads, but I don't know what to get." Their 12-year-old daughter had gotten her period. For the first time. Without Mom being there. Just Dad. After registering that it was only a *minor catastrophe* that this had happened while she was an ocean away, Wendy had him survey the supply drawer. She had had the "conversation" with her daughter a few months before and told her where to find things, but the boxes were empty, and her husband would need to replenish them. She texted him some photos for reference and called her daughter while he headed to the store. Father: mortified. Mother: anguished. Daughter: cool as a cucumber.

The many sides of guilt

As working mothers, we feel guilty when we leave our children in the morning or come home late in the evening. In our Thrive group, many of us travel extensively: grueling trips to Asia, Africa or Latin America are not unusual. We feel guilty coming home late on the average workday, and even more so as we dial in to check up on homework from Kuala Lumpur. We don't just worry about how our absence will affect our children, but we also feel guilty leaving our spouses to solo parent. And we have the same gnawing sense of inadequacy when we aren't able to find the time between trips to see our elderly parents or have to cancel on a friend for the umpteenth time due to work or travel. The guilt also cuts the other way: we may also feel guilty when we need to leave work early or when we have to cancel a work trip for personal reasons.

Sometimes the guilt is self-imposed, but we also absorb it from the world around us. Ursula von der Leyen, the impressive President of the European Commission, has shared a question she got when she had first become a minister. The interviewer asked her: "Have you chosen yet whether you are going to be a bad mother, or a bad minister?" This message is rarely put so bluntly, but it is often just below the surface.

Early on we found that the feelings of guilt were more acute for some than others in our group, and we wanted to unpack what made it easier for them. Often it had to do with the role models we grew up with. Wendy was one of the members least prone to guilt. Her parents had been amicably divorced when she was young, and she and her siblings lived with their working mother in Connecticut and spent every other weekend in New York City with their father. Their mother was a passionate sailor and more often than not, when the siblings were in New York, she would take off to go sailing, sometimes on day trips but often on overnights or even for race weeks. Well taken care of and exploring New York with their father on the weekends, the siblings could see the happiness and purpose that sailing gave to their mother. It also made it clear to them the value placed on independence and adventure.

In the day-to-day, Wendy's mother was unapologetic, even enthusiastic, about the kids needing to make their way home from school and settle into homework while she was still at work.

It was a fun adventure for the kids who never understood the stigma or downside of so-called "latchkey kids." At the same time, their mother never missed a call from the kids when she was at work, no matter how inane. For a time, she worked in a massive hangar where huge sails were constructed, and every time a child would call, she would have to traipse the length of a football field to pick up the single phone in the space, just to field a call about where the baking powder was (exactly where it should be) or what time the orthodontist appointment was (usually ten minutes prior). She (almost) always responded with patience and enthusiasm. Having that role model helped Wendy have the confidence that her children would be fine, even if she couldn't be there for every bump and bruise they got.

Our purpose matters

The lessons Thrive women took away from their conversations about guilt were important. First, our children need to see that the things that take us away from them are important and meaningful. It is not just a matter of going to work so that the bills can be paid and nice things can be purchased, but that when we leave home, we are going to do things that will make us better people, and make the world a better place. For Thrive women, because we all work in fields which have strong social impact, we have found that sharing with our children how our work will help others to live better lives, and not just how it puts food on our own table, has been a powerful way to help our kids get comfortable with our work. They also need to see that it brings us energy and fulfillment, and that it is normal and good for parents to have causes and passions beyond just their children, whether through work or other commitments.

Making sure our partners are sending the same messages is also critical. Lisa has always been grateful that her husband, Álvaro, consistently encourages her to take time for the activities where she finds purpose, meaning and fulfillment, and that he reinforces that to their daughter, Bella. Whether it was participating in Leadership San Francisco, attending Thrive retreats, going to book club or jazz singing lessons, he has always been supportive of her living the growth mindset, stretching and nurturing herself. One of their "Loving Couple Commandments," Be Your Best Self, encapsulates this idea and Álvaro's warm response taught her an important lesson in striving to live life to the fullest without guilt. For their daughter, it is also an important lesson that she will take into her own adulthood.

The good side of absence

The second lesson is to be unapologetic. Many of us have internalized the tropes about working moms somehow damaging their children. This seems to be especially so if we ourselves had stay-at-home mothers or difficult childhoods with two working parents. But research shows[40] that the opposite is true. Children with working mothers grow up just as happy as those who have stay-at-home mothers. Girls of working mothers are also more successful professionally than those with mothers at home. For boys, the effect of having a working mom on their professional success is negligible, but they are far more likely to have more equitable marriages with greater sharing of domestic responsibilities. So not only should we not give in to our fears that our absence will have long-term impacts on our children, but we should be proud that we are role modeling behaviors that will make the next generation even better at work-life balance.

Another benefit of absence is the deeper bonds that children form with their other caregivers. We have often observed how much stronger and more layered our husbands' relationships with our children are after we have been away for an extended period. Children become more resilient when they navigate the different rules (some big, some small) of different parents, and get to know their parents as more complete people when they are on their own. It is sometimes hard to come back and find the children are following different rules, but we should instead be appreciative that their bonds with fathers or other caregivers are deepening. If we can show gratitude for that, rather than frustration at our rules being bent, our families will become stronger.

Flip the narrative

Sometimes, we just need to flip the narrative, even if in the beginning we need to "fake it till we make it" so. Working mothers do themselves and their children a disservice when they over-apologize for their absence, or even use the well-worn "I wish I could stay but I have to go to work so that we can buy…" We have even had discussions about the implicit message it sends when we come home from a trip laden with guilt-induced gifts for our children. We have all had the experience of our children picking up on our own expressions of guilt and expertly using them as a weapon on us the next time around. Sometimes we *are* sorry, and we *do* wonder if we would do this job if we didn't have the mortgage to pay or college savings accounts to fill. But even so, we quickly reap benefits when we acknowledge our children's own concerns. And when we remove guilt from the equation and instead focus on the valuable opportunities they will have when we are away to deepen relationships with Dad or Grandma, and to grow independence and resilience. There is power in changing the narrative in our head and communicating a new storyline to our family.

Acknowledge the challenge

Of course, not all guilt can be waved away. We're not talking about forgetting the bake-sale contribution or arriving last to parent pick-up. It's about more serious stuff, where our choices really could have a lasting impact on our children. For example, we may not realize it when a child is facing anxiety or a mental health crisis, only to see the symptoms grow while we are away on a work trip. Or we may lose our temper more than we like, even when we know it will have the opposite of the desired effect. In these cases, we may have regrets, and they can be painful. They are also often intertwined with many of our own narratives from our childhood, our parents, and our hopes and dreams for our children, and our confidence (or lack thereof) of our own parenting skills. It can be difficult to unpack it all, but it is important to try to understand and own our failures, forgive ourselves but work to get better next time. Our children can learn a lot also if they see us acknowledge that we are not perfect and aspire to do better. If we can learn and not repeat the mistakes of the past, we can move forward. Sometimes it is simply recommitting to greater focus and listening to our children; other times it is allocating real time to address their emotional and physical needs; still other times we need to push the pause button elsewhere and carve out time for ourselves to make sure we can provide the emotional support they need.

The guilt sandwich: aging parents and young children

Some Thrive members associate guilt less with our children than with our own parents or in-laws. Having had children later, we find ourselves in a guilt sandwich, worried about how we are not being good enough mothers, and also not doing enough to support our aging parents as they go from helping us with our busy lives, to needing our help as they age. As they get older, time becomes more precious with them but also more demanding, and we struggle to strike the right balance. When our parents live far away, the guilt has even more dimensions. For some of us, during the COVID-19 pandemic, the isolation and daily threat to our parents' health made the waves of guilt into tsunamis.

We are learning as we go, but it seems to be that when we can engage with our aging parents, without judgment, wherever they are at a given moment, is when we can spark joy. As hard as it is for our parents to practice the letting go that is required as they age, it is difficult for us too to let go of our old expectations of our parents. Finding ways to bridge the gap is essential, whether it is reading or talking to them on a Zoom call or helping them connect with an old friend or hobby – or even their life story.

In Wendy's case, her father lived in New York and had had a series of minor strokes and ill health when COVID-19 hit. She had a gnawing feeling that a door was closing to share meaningful time together. He had been working on a memoire for years but as his memory started to deteriorate, it was jeopardizing this legacy project. With the book nearing completion, Wendy decided to take it on as a "COVID-19 project" to help him get it past the finish line. The result was days and nights of incredible discussions with her father about the amazing episodes in his life that he had written about and needed refining. The stories were incredible: coming of age in the Southern California of the Beach Boys; being present during Bloody Sunday in Selma, Alabama; Flying B-52 bombers during the Cold War; working on the Apollo rocket that landed the first men on the moon; pioneering Affirmative Action work in NYC in the '80s; reforming the economies of the former Soviet Union in the '90s; and coming home to see the Twin Towers fall outside his apartment windows. The time turned out to be precious and the resulting book, *The Last Leather Helmets*, has helped him reach out to friends and family that might have otherwise been lost to him. This time spent together, with a common focus and a common passion – a gift of COVID-19 in many ways – was precious.

It is natural to feel guilty when we have to choose between so many things that are priorities. Often, like Sophie's Choice, it seems like a no-win situation. In the end we have to trust that our choices will be the right ones, most of the time, and be willing to acknowledge and forgive ourselves when they are not. Our children will be resilient, our parents will still love us, and we will always be able to do better next time.

Taking Care of Ourselves: Health, Happiness and Letting Go

Thrive women often feel like jugglers in a circus. With so many competing demands on our time between intense days at work, a vibrant home life, and our other passions, it often feels hard to find time to rest and recharge personally. We have come to see the wisdom in the flight attendant's admonishment: "in case of emergency, put on your own oxygen mask first." Especially as we age, taking care of ourselves becomes an investment in the future, an investment that doesn't just benefit ourselves, but benefits our families, our work and our communities. We've each had wake-up calls reminding us that we only have one life, one body, one mind. If we don't take care of ourselves, we will not be able to take care of others. These life lessons have inspired us to ask questions like: How can we set a new normal of physical and mental health? Are we taking time to celebrate and bring gratitude into our lives? When is good, good enough?

Setting our Healthy New Normal

Take care of our body: it's the only place you have to live.
—Jim Rohn

Lisa experienced a classic wake-up call the day before she was to leave for Paris to attend the pivotal United Nations event known as COP-21 in December 2015 – when 125 governments from around the world committed to do their part to fight climate change. Lisa had a lingering winter cough whenever she laughed and thought it best to get it checked out before leaving. Still new to DC, she didn't have a doctor who knew her, so she signed up for the first available appointment that afternoon in a local clinic. When the nurse practitioner asked what the problem was, Lisa put her hand on her chest and said she was having pain there and trouble breathing. The next thing she knew, she was hooked up to an EKG for the first time in her life. The next few minutes were a blur. A paramedic team was soon towering over her, whisking her onto a stretcher and into an ambulance waiting in the now heavy traffic just blocks from the White House. She was shocked to hear that there was something irregular with her heart and that she needed to be seen urgently in a hospital. In the hours that followed, Lisa imagined the worst. But by the time Lisa's husband reached her, the heart scare was officially over. She was diagnosed with a bad case of bronchitis.

Listening to our "lifequakes"

While Lisa's bronchitis cleared up quickly, the shock of those few hours has had a long-lasting impact on how she lives her life. The term "lifequake" was coined by Bruce Feiler to describe the massive changes in our lives that lead to a life transition.[41] There are endless triggers for a so-called "lifequake" but perhaps the most common is the health scare. The bronchitis episode was such a lifequake for Lisa. She first cycled through a range of emotions – relief that the issue was manageable, gratitude for access to fast medical attention, anger at the astronomical medical bill caused by the false alarm, and regret to miss what was sure to be a historic event. But ultimately, Lisa was left with a sense of *carpe diem*. None of us know what may happen health-wise or what's lurking around the corner. The only thing we can do is to invest in our health, live each day to the fullest and avoid the potential for regret.

As working parents, it's so easy to go on autopilot and push ourselves hard day after day taking care of everyone around us except ourselves. In the end, whether they are as dramatic as being rushed to the emergency room or something more benign like a conversation with a loved one or a colleague, the wake-up calls are a gift. They give us the chance to see our lives more clearly. They give us the impetus to stop taking our lives for granted. And they give us the push we may need to take back the steering wheels of our lives so that we prioritize our own wellbeing.

COVID-19 put the focus on our health and safety front and center, leading all of us to reevaluate the daily choices we make. As work and life blurred in the midst of the pandemic, and as it became harder to carve out time for self-care, many of us and our colleagues experienced extraordinary levels of stress, gained weight, faced depression and even burnout. We learned to recognize the telltale signs of burnout in ourselves and others – like catastrophizing, exhaustion, insomnia, irritability, feeling helpless, and not finding joy in the things that would typically bring a smile – and to try to take action before it can set in.[42] One of the silver linings was becoming more sensitive to these signs and what to do about them which we now realize can crop up with people working in our 24/7 culture. At a particular personal low point a few months into the pandemic, Lisa was grateful when a colleague rang her up after a team call to ask the question, "Are you okay?" It was a gift that her colleague took the time to recognize that she wasn't acting like her motivated, resilient self and to bring it to her attention. This gave Lisa the chance to reflect herself and take some days off to recharge before pushing herself to the brink.

Adjusting through life stages

We have found noticeable changes to our bodies as we've moved into our forties and fifties. Aching joints after we exercise. Waking up in the middle of the night and taking an hour to get back to sleep. Graduating to bi-focal contact lenses. Tearing a meniscus after years of running. The predictable list goes on and on. What we realized individually and collectively is that we need to listen to our bodies, accept that at every age we need to adjust, and build the habits early on that will serve us well as we move forward.

As Wendy neared 40, with three children under three and heading back to work full time, she realized something had to give. She previously had the enviable ability to catch a few hours of sleep pretty much anywhere or any time, wake up and be fully functional. Her natural tendency was to power through work after the kids went to bed and stay up past midnight multiple times a week. This pattern was fine in her twenties but her body and mind were not as forgiving as she moved into her forties, especially when she needed to be up early to get the kids to school or an early meeting, or when her sleep was interrupted during the night. She found that she needed to make specific commitments to herself about sleep, which meant shedding her "night owl" approach (most of the time) and shifting to an "earlier to sleep, earlier to rise" schedule. It can be hard to fight the urge to work late into the night or to binge watch the latest on Netflix, but we've found that there is really no substitute for a good night sleep and that shifting the clock to have more productive mornings really makes a difference.

Why putting our mask on first is actually selfless

For Monica, the wake-up call came one day in her forties with a tingling in her arm that got progressively worse. Because her mother had died young and her family had a history of heart disease and hypertension, she has always been acutely aware of the very real potential consequences of poor health. She went to a series of specialists who couldn't figure out what was wrong. After a battery of MRI, EKG and stress tests, she discovered that she had severe scoliosis that was never picked up in all those high school exams. Then came multiple interventions by a chiropractor, physical therapist and acupuncturist (by far the most effective).

In the end, Monica found her path to whole body "wellness" while on an extended stay in South Africa. The answer? Shifting from a heavy jogging schedule to balanced workouts with more strength training, more sleep, drinking more glasses of water each day, unplugging at night and on the weekends, and regular meditation practice. She also got into the habit of carving out 20–30 minutes each morning before the kids got up. A good morning would start with a 7–10-minute meditation (Calm became her app of choice); 7–10 minutes of non-work reading and 10 minutes of journaling. What began as a "rigid" 30 minutes softened to allow some exercise like yoga or jogging – which would also change her physiology and framing for the day. Rather than feeling guilty for taking "me" time, she found the practice helped her in her attempts to silence her "inner critic" and show up more fully and positively for those around her – at home and at work. The big "aha"? How important it is to treat ailments holistically and not assume that the cause of a health problem is the obvious surface one but to stay curious about uncovering the true source.

In some way, Monica's shift from jogging to strength training has been a metaphor for an important shift in her mindset: slow and steady wins the race. The shift has worked wonders. Consciously building our own personal new normal is all about investing the time upfront to develop the habits that are "built to last" – to quote Jerry Porras' famous book.[43] The result? Monica found that she could feel her body running differently than it used to and recovery times were shorter.

A priceless investment: cognitive reserve

On one of their "walk and talks" around the lush trails of Rock Creek Park in DC surrounded by bikers, runners, cars and the occasional deer, Wendy and Lisa talked about aging. Wendy's mother, who had had her children in her early 20s, was still joining the family's grueling summer hikes with her children and nine grandchildren well into her 60s. Wendy mused about how much older she would be when her kids had their own kids. It dawned on her that her health was not just a here and now issue, but an investment in that future. They agreed to help each other cultivate the habits and make time to build strength as well as physical and mental reserves for the long-term. We want not just to be active in our 40s and 50s, but lay the groundwork so that we can do so into our 60s and 70s.

The idea of applying this reserve concept to our physical and even mental health is powerful and attractive. Two years after Lisa's luckily benign pre-COP21 wake-up call, she found herself in another doctor's office. This time it was an orthopedic surgeon. After more than twenty years of waking up to morning runs multiple times per week, Lisa's right knee suddenly started to smart and make clicking sounds on every step. For her, running was her happy, quiet place. Part of her morning routine to clear her mind with the meditative rhythm of repetitive steps. And a place to compose thoughts, rehearse speeches, or mull over conversations. The MRI had picked up a torn meniscus, a very common runner's injury.

Lisa asked the highly recommended orthopedist about the likely causes and what she could do about it. Dissatisfied with his "wear and tear" diagnosis – which she heard as "you are getting old and it's all downhill from here" – she pushed for something more scientific, like a certain gait that could be altered. Months later when her knee started to heal as a result of more variety in her exercise routine (spin classes and bike rides) and her ego started to mend, Lisa reset her perspective. Rather than feel sorry for herself and imagine her body in irreversible decline, she would consciously take steps to set a new normal of physical and mental health, a reserve, so that the future declines would be coming from a much higher baseline.

Building reserves is not just a physical issue, but also a mental one. Lisa's husband, Álvaro, CEO and Editor-in-chief of SharpBrains,[44] has impressed upon her the importance of building cognitive, emotional, neural, and mental resilience by cultivating lifelong neuroplasticity. Just as we develop cardio capacity, muscles and core strength by doing circuit training and a range of physical exercises, we build brain reserves with healthy nutrition, physical and cognitive exercise, stress regulation, curiosity and lifelong learning. The cognitive reserve itself is made up of neurons and the strongest, most efficient connections between them. These connections are patiently built day after day, year after year. Studies have shown that having a larger cognitive reserve serves as a "buffer" that helps people substantially delay symptoms of dementia even when Alzheimer's markers are physically present in their brain.

Research also shows that novelty, variety and challenge are key ingredients to strengthen neural pathways. Exercise helps with the generation of new neurons and regulating stress helps protect those new neurons. In addition, the more we practice something, the more we strengthen neural connections, making them resilient and longer lasting.[45] It turns out that one of the most rewarding and powerful ways to stimulate our brain and build up our cognitive reserves is to cultivate a beginner's mind. There's been an observed uptick in learning during the COVID-19 pandemic as enrollments spiked on a wide range of topics from learning Spanish on Duolingo to baking on Tik Tok, or juggling on Masterclass.[46] The more we learn and challenge ourselves, the more we create new neurons and fortify their connections. Neuroplasticity continues for our entire life. The earlier we start, the better, but it's never too late to start.

Arianna Huffington shines a light on the damage the "all-out culture" can do in her book *Thrive*, a wake-up call for our generation to leave space for breathing, sleeping and exercising in our busy lives.[47] For others, the space is created by taking time to reset with quick breathing exercises, visualizations, or walks while at work. Drawing from his knowledge of neuroscience and how to apply its lessons to our daily lives, Lisa's husband taught her a simple but powerful visualization exercise that takes only five seconds and can entirely change the mood. The way to do the "five fingers" exercise is to touch your thumb to each finger and to visualize something different with each finger. A moment of physical exertion. A loving exchange. An unexpected gift. A beautiful landscape. Another version is to call up the five senses with each finger. The more complex our lives are, the more we realize that there are simple things that can ground us and help us to be more resilient. Building these mental muscles and responses to stress are critical skills. They are as valid in preparing for a stressful meeting as they are in finding a way to deal with a parent's health challenge or a child's insouciance.

Help our communities help us

It is difficult to remain healthy when we are in an unhealthy environment, whether it be at work or at home. Early in the pandemic, there was a cascade of shutdowns globally, as governments around the world sought to contain the virus. Lisa found that the sense of losing control was palpable among team members from all corners of the globe, and it was compounding her own anxieties. She found solace in doing ten-minute guided meditations on her phone using her favorite Headspace app – a birthday present from her husband who deeply understands the power of now. One day, she decided to share this with her team. She started her work calls, even thirty-minute ones, with a quick, sixty second, guided meditation. Though she did not have any training, she overcame her hesitation seeing how stressed her colleagues were by the dramatic changes they were facing. While the exercise took only one minute, she saw from the reactions of colleagues how useful it was to create a space free of the whirling movies in our minds. Instead of diverting time from the pressing needs of work, it turned out that taking a few moments of calm at the start of calls had the opposite effect. Creating space to center and clear the non-stop distractions of the pandemic made it more possible to focus and be productive.

We found that something else also contributed to the mental health of our families and neighbors during the pandemic. Our furry little friends. There's nothing quite like the unbridled enthusiasm of a dog when you walk in the room or she wakes up from a nap. Wendy got wise to this many years ago and saw how her family's dog was a great source of love and stress relief for everyone in the household. After what seemed like a ten-year campaign by their daughter, it took moving to Florida, having a backyard, and a global pandemic for Lisa and Álvaro to agree to bring a dog home. They were not disappointed. Ever since, they have been pleasantly surprised at how much joy and laughter is sparked by their "baby dog." In addition to demonstrating how persistence pays off in the end, their dog has also provided a good excuse to get out of the house even when it felt easier to stay inside during COVID-19.

When we share the basics of meditation or yoga with our children, find ways to get our husbands to enjoy eating healthier, take time to walk and talk with a colleague, take a family dog walk around the neighborhood, or do a bootcamp with a friend, we are reinforcing our own healthy community and support network. In the end, our healthy habits make us feel more sustained, and connecting those habits to our friends and family makes them more sustainable.

There's always a blue sky above

One of the most reassuring things about flying in an airplane is that when we get through a turbulent climb through the clouds, we always eventually break through to the blue sky or a starry night. No matter how thick the clouds, there is always a beautiful sky above. A coach of Lisa's shared this beautiful metaphor with her which resonated strongly given how many times she has flown and noticed the same thing. When things are turbulent in the heat of the moment, whether with kids or at work, we have found that it can be quite reassuring and grounding to remember that there's always a blue sky above and that if we're persistent, we will break through the cloud cover.

Covid-19 was a wake-up call for many of us about just how precious our life and our health is. It was a stark reminder that as leaders and as parents, our first responsibility is our duty of care, how we steward and nurture the people in our proverbial gardens. The thought of setting a new normal is a powerful motivator for us, allowing us to keep the blue sky in our minds even on the cloudiest days. Whether it be cultivating habits of exercise, meditation, more sleep, learning, stretching, or just taking time to pause, we are able to reconnect to that inner compass and replenish our reserves. As professional coach Jerry Colonna posits in Reboot, "I refuse to conspire in my own diminishment. I make life choices that let me bring my best self forward."

Taking Time for Fun, Celebration and Gratitude

Be thankful for what you have: you'll end up having more. If you concentrate on what you don't have, you will never, ever have enough.
—Oprah Winfrey

The summer before the world shut down, Monica and her husband were contemplating how to celebrate a milestone birthday and their fifteenth wedding anniversary. After reflecting on what kind of commemoration would feel most fitting, whether it would be adults only or if they should organize separate events – they decided that what would make them happiest was to be in a beautiful setting, with dear friends and their kids gathered from different corners of the globe. After many searches on VRBO, they found a thirteenth-century villa in a rural corner of Spain that was perfect in its simplicity and communal feeling. Two hours from Barcelona, the place had open spaces for kids to run around and play games in, a pool for cooling down on hot summer days, a huge outdoor *parilla* to grill, and a farm table where everyone could eat and linger into the night. Some days, breakfast would turn into lunch, punctuated by siestas and then dinner, while other days the group would pile into a van to go to the beach or the nearby village. Mostly, the days consisted of good food and good conversations, kids buzzing about from soccer pitch to pool, and a strong dose of gratitude.

The name of the Catalan castle – *Mas Sunyer* – became a WhatsApp group where the friends who had joined in the festivities continued to share travel adventures and stories of carving time out to take in life's simplest pleasures. We consciously try to cultivate this habit of celebrating among the Thrive group members. Together, we have celebrated big milestones like Lisa and her husband's re-committing their marriage vows in honor of their tenth wedding anniversary and Wendy's fiftieth birthday with a girls-only yoga retreat in Mexico. We also celebrate new jobs, successful conferences, and getting through health scares with a meal, a walk and talk, or champagne. This practice of not only stocktaking but actively celebrating milestones, recognizing life's blessings, and re-affirming priorities – a loving supportive spouse, healthy curious kids, deep friendships, the financial wherewithal to plan a getaway or host a party – has become something we share with the Thrive group.

New traditions

While traditions bind us over time, celebrations allow us to commemorate sometimes once-in-a-lifetime milestones and create new memories with those we care about. After a year of Zoom celebrations, we can say with all candor, they'll do in a pinch, but it is just not the same as being together eating and hugging in person.

The Thrive women come from a variety of religious traditions, but we all value the big and small traditions that mark the passage of time, prompt us to pause, enjoy each other's company and find common ground. A year of COVID-19 brought home how much we rely on our Thanksgivings with grandparents, summer get-togethers with cousins, Shabbat dinner with close friends, school graduations, reunions, and even fourth of July picnics with neighbors.

At the most basic level, we try to keep nightly dinners "sacred" with no electronics at the table and no excuses for not joining (cleanup is a less beloved, but no less important tradition!). Wendy's family has a tradition where a knife is spun at dinner and whoever it lands on shares their "favorite thing of the day" or "a rose and a thorn." With teenagers or even pre-teens at the table, eyes may roll, but it is usually good for an interesting story or two. The Sabbath gives some time for taking a mindful pause at the end of the week to reflect and give thanks. The regular get-togethers take different forms, such as a weekly date night with a partner or a dad's night out, but they are all sacred times that serve a similar purpose. All of these traditions bring us closer together with our loved ones and give everyone involved a feeling of belonging and connection. For our children, they create deep memories and bonds that they will carry forward to their own friends and families like we have to ours.

Spontaneous joy

At its most basic level, however, the key to finding time, each day, including "transitions,"[48] is to literally and figuratively just put down one's phone, one's work hotline, and pause to play and talk with kids and partners. When Wendy's kids were young, before she could even put down her bag from a day at work, her kids would race down the stairs screaming with delight and jump on top of her, vying with each other for her love and attention. Within minutes, they'd be upstairs in the playroom having a dance party (Happy, Dynamite and Dancing Queen were the family favorites). Soon enough, dinner would have to be made, baths taken, PJs put on and bedtime stories read. After sleep, rooms and dishes got tidied and if there was any gas in the tank, an hour or two of work before turning in. But oh, the dance parties! They could have been 10 minutes or a half hour, but they made all the difference.

Unfortunately, dance parties seem to lose their appeal at some point and teenagers are more likely to run *from* us rather than run to *us* when we come home from work, but the memories still bind. The fun may shift to less frequent and more mellow endeavors – a board game, a round of cards, jumping into the pool, taking a ski day, or watching a favorite show together – but the essence is the same. Important for our child, yes, but maybe even more important for the parents' wellbeing.

The satisfaction "set point"

There are many different theories on what it takes to be happy, with religious leaders, social scientists, psychologists and sport coaches all having their views. A weekly column in *The Atlantic* by Arthur Brooks called "How to Build a Life," explores many aspects of the highly desired state.[49] On the one hand, he talks about the role of genetics in determining our "set point" for subjective wellbeing, the baseline we always seem to return to after events sway our mood. On the other, he explores how the combination of relationships, work that gives us a sense of purpose, and an acceptance of dimensions beyond what we can see together to form habits that fuel a deep sense of satisfaction.

One of the core practices in Buddhism is the notion of letting go of the wants that are stoked by our consumer, always-on culture and focusing on the little things in daily life – the scent of a rose, a smile on our children's faces, looking up at a tree canopy. The Dalai Lama famously said, "We need to learn how to want what we have, not to have what we want, in order to get steady and stable Happiness."[50] The more we chase after it, the more elusive it can become. In a similar vein, a lesson from a Buddhist monk has stayed with Lisa and her husband. He told a simple parable about a fly buzzing around a room. The more the people chased after the fly, the more aggravated they got (apparently, they could not channel Mr. Miyagi in *The Karate Kid*). Then someone had the idea to open the window. The fly eventually flew out of the room, leaving them in peace. This approach can be applied to meditation. If we can open the windows in our mind and let our thoughts, anxieties, distractions wander out on their own, we can be more present in the moment with ourselves and our family.

With small children, it becomes almost inconceivable to take time out to cultivate a hobby or passion that doesn't involve the kids, but as time goes on the impossible becomes possible again. When she was newly married in San Francisco, Lisa was inspired to pick up a hobby she'd loved since she was in her high school choir, singing outside of the shower. She took jazz singing lessons for a few years, even singing her favorite Diana Krall song at the parties on her and Álvaro "Worldwide Wedding Tour." After a hiatus when her daughter was young, she and her best friend from high school, who was actually in that original school choir, found a place to take lessons and sing jazz again in DC. No matter how busy a day she's having, it's better – for her and everyone she is with – after she gets into the flow of singing a new jazz song or learning to scat.

Remembering to make time for fun

Though Monica was an active parent when her kids were little, she often wondered if she was missing out on too many moments in their lives. Her daughter captured it perfectly one day after school, when her brother asked if Mom would come outside and play ball. Before she could answer – with dinner prep waiting – her daughter stated authoritatively: "Don't you know? Daddy plays. Mommy works."

The innocent observation stopped Monica in her tracks and forced her to reflect on the fact that, apparently, she wasn't the "fun parent." Even when she was being present with her kids, she was more likely to be discussing school, the recent soccer game or the plans for the weekend. Finding time for fun with her kids and her husband often seemed to fall off the schedule.

Even with the best intentions, there are inevitably times when our cup overfloweth, and not in a good way. Life with an intense job, children, parents and other obligations can force many things onto the back burner if it stays on the menu at all. If the things that make us laugh and enjoy life and enjoy our kids' childhoods are the things that are being put on the back burner, we need to re-prioritize.

Taking a step back, Monica realized she was at a crossroads in her career and at home. She had successfully convinced her corporate sponsor to spin off the in-house fund she had launched after her twins were born, and there were major institutional investors stepping up to anchor the new third-party fund. She had been "leaning in" at work, busy with the negotiations on the new fund, finding a business partner with more traditional venture experience, and the ongoing work of the existing fund. At home, her twins were four and starting school full time and her aunts who had traveled from Peru to help care for the kids were getting ready to return home to their own families. She found support through the local university jobs board, hiring a "home helper" to help the kids with their after-school schedule, get dinner on the table, picking up milk at the store, or pitching in around the house. Because the "home helpers" were students, there was always the understanding that school came first – so sometimes these assignments would fall back on Monica and her husband. But the extra set of hands meant more time for playing soccer and games, date nights, girlfriend gatherings and self-care.

Another key to "finding time" was to lock in morning time for journaling, meditating and running. The irony that Monica found if she took *more* time for herself, she could actually create *greater* capacity to enjoy time with others. Just like the taxi driver who once cautioned Monica that "Sometimes we have to go slow to go fast," a more considered, deliberate approach allows one to reach their desired outcomes more quickly than a frenzied, "urgent" pace. That quiet, focused time helped Monica set her intentions and priorities, and delegate or set aside the work that she couldn't get to but that was less important than her "fun time" or other activities that gave her joy.

The almost magical notion of making time by spending time wisely struck a chord with Thrive women. Most feel that on a typical day, every time they cross a task off the to-do list, three more are added, each seemingly more essential than the last. Things that bring personal joy often seem to sit at the bottom of the list. Like the adage that the time needed to complete a task will stretch to the time set aside for it, we find that carving out time to dance with our kids, or kick a soccer ball does not change what gets done on our to-do list. But it does something else. When we give ourselves permission to relax and enjoy life with those around us, we find we are refreshed and have a new energy to put into the rest of our day.

As a year of lockdown showed us, even if we find our fun in the little things – a quick game of cards, watching a show side-by-side, having a birthday Zoom call, or cultivating a new hobby – it nourishes us for all the other, not so fun times.

Gratitude in the time of COVID-19

Several years ago, Lisa gave Wendy and Monica a gratitude journal, following a conversation where they realized in their busy lives, they often failed to appreciate all the good in their lives. The simple act of journaling three things each day that they were grateful for was uplifting. In some ways COVID-19 focused us even more acutely on the saving grace of simple pleasures – whether baking bread, eating a slow lunch with our families, or walks with our neighbors. Most of the Thrive women were lucky enough to be spared infection, were able to work from home along with their spouses during the pandemic and had kids old enough to manage their schoolwork and self-care on their own. We frequently took stock of how lucky we were, especially in light of very real inequalities and inequities that COVID-19 laid bare. Finding ways to share our gratitude and give back – through our work and in our personal lives – where we can, has become more important than ever.

Perfection Is the Enemy of the Good

Perfectionism is a 20 ton shield we carry around hoping that it will keep us from getting hurt – when in truth, it keeps us from being seen and taking flight.
—Brené Brown

When the world shut down for COVID-19, many of us had the idea that it might create space in our lives to do more of what we yearned to do but could not find the time for. We eagerly stacked our bed stands with literature to learn more about the world; explanations of pandemics to try to understand what was happening; treatises on feminism, the future of work and innovation to bolster our respective professional bonafides; cookbooks, gardening books, parenting tips and hiking guides to make our COVID-19-based home lives more fruitful. When a child came out as gay, books on LGBTQ were added. When George Floyd was killed, we downloaded books on white privilege and systemic injustice. Then, more books to understand and protect ourselves and our loved ones from the health crises in our lives: COVID-19, dementia, menopause, disability. Eventually, maybe inevitably, books on gratitude, vulnerability and spirituality.

Our overloaded bed stands, Kindle libraries and podcasts became metaphors for our desire to become the best versions of ourselves. Ultimately, as they sat partially unread, they became a testament to the fact that we cannot possibly do it all.

Dropping the ball: the futility of trying to have it all

Most of the women of Thrive are juggling demanding careers, kids, spouses, homes and any number of other obligations. In a group of ambitious women who have made important strides professionally, it will be no surprise to learn that we are often very hard on ourselves. The subtext is that we believe we are not measuring up in some part of our lives – as an absentee mom, as a distracted leader, as a neglectful daughter, as a fair-weather friend. No matter how hard we tried to rationalize, we somehow were not "good enough." The uncolored part of our wheel could be read as always "lacking" somewhere. Too often, that leads us to think that we should be more and do more. It is so easy to look at someone else's Instagram page, LinkedIn postings, or holiday card and feel inadequate. Exotic vacations, fun parties, adventurous outings, insightful tweets, well-deserved promotions, celebrations of big accomplishments.

We have often worn our busy-ness as a badge of honor. One of the silver linings of the pandemic was to discover how many things we thought essential are actually not. Many of those formerly known as essential things that kept us so busy have been replaced by lower-key alternatives. A weekend at home with no sports tournaments for the kids – not so bad. Discovering a town in driving distance from home versus flying abroad for vacation – a more accessible surprise. Shopping in an outfit we *might* have also slept in – no longer so embarrassing. At the same time, we started wondering if we should be doing more of other things. Should I be converting my backyard into a garden like my neighbor? Maybe it would be good to take up beekeeping like my siblings? Why am I not baking bread each day like my friend? Or... why not write a book like my mentor? Okay, we fell for that one: old habits die hard.

In a great conversation about "dropping the ball" with Tiffany Dufu, Sheryl Sandburg said it well: "All of us are walking around with feelings of inadequacy, as if we're not doing enough, but what we're expecting ourselves to do is not humanly possible."[51] Often these expectations are reinforced by external perceptions or a "disease to please." Thrive women encourage each other to look inward, get clear on goals and priorities, and then strive healthily. As we do this it becomes easier to let go of the things that may seem necessary but are not giving us joy, become comfortable with imperfection, and build reserves to manage the ebbs and flows of life.

Trust fall

Having the flexibility to say no to some things so we can focus on what is important does not just happen. While we would like to say that we gracefully pirouette from the demanding boss to the needy child to the important moment of celebration, some days we are just lunging from crisis to crisis as the needs present themselves. In the rare times we feel like we have successfully dodged a bullet, passed the baton, juggled the balls, and gotten a slam dunk – all in a day's work, it is invariably because of the people who've got our back. We all rely on people who can take over for us when something needs to give: other moms who can take our children when there is an emergency at work; our colleagues who will take our shift because we've done it for them in the past; a boss who allows a deliverable to drop when there is just too much on our plate; a spouse who will drop everything when we need to tend to an ailing parent; a friend who will suspend judgment when a fun outing needs to be canceled; and even children who are resilient enough to roll with it when a performance or game is missed. This is what Hillary Clinton was talking about when she said, "It takes a village to raise a child." We would just add that it takes a village to raise a child, *lean in at work and still thrive*. Tiffany Dufu points out that we need to "Lean in with scaffolding... When we can create an ecosystem of support, villages of support, it's not so scary to lean in because we know if we fall somebody is going to catch us."[52]

Building goodwill so that these impositions are met with smiles and not gritted teeth is an important piece of this puzzle. In our experience, the best way to do this is to pay it forward, knowing that if we can put in the extra effort up front it will be rewarded down the road. The friend who knows we have been and will be there for her; the boss who knows that we will always deliver 110% if we can, and that if we cannot, it is for real; our spouse who knows that it is a two-way street and that if we need our girls' nights, he gets his poker nights. Finding ways to be generous and go the extra mile for the people that are important in our life pays back in spades when we need to pull back on one part of our life to focus on another.

Engaging (then appeasing) the inner critic

The other piece of the puzzle is self-forgiveness. It is an old trope that when we believe we are not doing enough, it is really the fear that we are not good enough, accomplished enough, or successful enough. In some cases, we realize that there really are trade-offs that are painful and regrets if we do not live our priorities. Many Thrive women have internalized Martha Stewart expectations of "doing it all" – over-committing on work and home responsibilities instead of making requests to recontract and rebalance. These missteps and corresponding disappointments are part of the journey. The key is to own them, reflect on the learnings, and turn the page – rather than berate ourselves. Listening to the inner voice that says – to take a break, refuel – rather than always rallying to please, perfect, and perform is a first step. There is always another mountain to climb. Actually, there is an unlimited number of mountains to climb to prove our worth. It is essential to forgive ourselves when we decide not to climb a mountain, or when we get halfway up and decide to stop.

Often self-care creates internal confusion or conflict among working moms, as it seems indulgent. Understanding the message of the self-critic – the voice of some inner part that is anxious, alienated, alone – allows one to engage these dissatisfied parts of ourselves empathetically and with compassion, rather than shame or blame.[53] Put another way, trying to *understand* why we have had challenges changing a habit or reaching a goal (rather than berating ourselves for failing) often leads to insights on small shifts we can make, new patterns that move us forward in a more balanced, integrated way. Thrive, too, has helped identify those (self) saboteurs quickly and change the self-talk.

And what about that nagging feeling that there is still more self-improvement to do? Pausing and reflecting whether the motivation is internal (healthy striving) or external (pleasing and perfecting to avoid judgment)[54] is critical – as is taking the long-view. Who is to say this is the year we need to nab that promotion, become a ninja in bed and take up beekeeping? There are plenty of good ideas for a bucket list when there is more time or urgency. Instead of dwelling on whether we measure up, we can focus on celebrating our friends who manage to do those things, while acknowledging that it is a beautiful dream that we can always do later.

Ditching drudgery in exchange for joy

Having agency means celebrating the things we choose to do and being grateful that we also can "just say no" (to paraphrase another First Lady). Just like Mari Kondo implores us to only hold on to objects that give us joy,[55] we need to proudly curate our obligations as well to maximize joy. The "simplify and focus" message of her best-selling book and similar business books like *Essentialism*[56] became the topic of many a Thrive lunch: drawing boundaries, saying no and sticking to routines. Rather than trying to "have it all" – we tried to focus on taking stock of what was already within our reach, focusing on priorities and what brought us joy.

Is there a conflict here? Yes. We often do things that we may not be excited about because we feel like we should, precisely because we want to build goodwill at work and deepen relationships with family and friends in our community – all part of the scaffolding we rely on. This juggling is one of the hardest parts of the balancing act: How do we make sure we're paying attention to our own internal reserves and self-care as well as the needs of others? How do we set boundaries and say "no" more often when we think we need to recalibrate? Here is where the agility of the wheel and personal agency comes in. What we have seen work amongst our Thrive members is going all-in to generously include others in the things that give us joy, which gives us room to gracefully decline getting dragged into activities that sap us. Often, starting with the former helps us evade the latter. Piling a few extra neighborhood kids into the minivan when heading to the park; managing a long weekend with the kids while hubby is on a "mantastic" getaway; or going the extra mile to polish a colleague's paper. For some of us, these are enjoyable activities that will also earn us a "get out of jail free card" to play later. What is important is that we proactively look for ways to pay it forward that also give us joy. For us these opportunities for generosity have also been the moments that have forged our closest and most meaningful relationships.

Appreciating the pause

Finally, one of the things COVID-19 has taught us is that there is also beauty in the white spaces, the down time we have to let things happen and evolve. It is hard to know how to value that time when life is busy, and the mountains are calling. Weekends without carpools, unmonitored time in the home office; vacations without travel. It begs an almost existential question of what it means to thrive if the "busy-ness" becomes optional and we get to redefine what is important. It has been interesting to see how we fill that time during the COVID-19 pandemic. Do we find other "home-friendly" projects to fill our days; or do we deliberately leave space for discovery, happenstance and the impromptu moments. We are experimenting with new ways of resting, striving, refueling, and balancing. The ebb and flow of different components of the wheel is sometimes an imperfect alchemy, like switching up a recipe by changing the mix of ingredients. It doesn't always turn out perfectly, but as Brene Brown reminds us, "the magic is in the mess."

Cultivating Intentional Communities

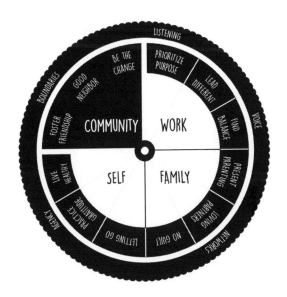

One of the most fundamental beliefs that anchors the women in Thrive is that our own success and wellbeing depends so much on our connectedness to our friends, our communities, and our world. For us to thrive, they must thrive as well. We are sometimes the givers, sometimes the takers, and sometimes the makers in our communities. This engagement is a fundamental element of what makes us who we are, helps us grow, and fulfills us. Most of the Thrive women live far away from the families, friends and communities where we grew up. We have faced both the challenges and joys of seeking and finding those people and places where we feel we belong, can be supported and challenged, and where we can contribute. The commitments we make to these people and places can be the best investments we make in our own and our families' lives and futures. Yet doing so with intentionality requires constant questioning and adjustments. We wonder how, in our busy lives, we can cultivate a strong and supportive network of friends that will bolster and fulfill us through our ups and downs. We consider how to find communities and experiences that will enable our families to create deep ties, a secure sense of belonging, but also an excitement to engage beyond our tribe. Finally, we wonder how we can be agents of change, to use our abilities, our example and our voices to cultivate a better world.

Building a Wolfpack

I come as one but, I stand as ten thousand.

—Maya Angelou

Lisa's daughter was around five weeks old in spring 2008 and crying loudly as she left the house. It was the first time Lisa had left her daughter in the care of her husband in their beautiful one-bedroom walk up. She had been reluctant to go, but with her husband's encouragement she stepped out the door. As she walked up one of San Francisco's iconic roller-coaster streets with distant views of the Bay, she could feel the anxious tug of separation alongside the elation of finally doing something for herself. Her destination was a gathering of half a dozen close friends in a house perched in the Berkeley hills. The friends called themselves Moms in Sustainability, or MOMSE, and got together monthly to connect and support each other as new mothers and career women. It truly would have been enough to just have an "adult" conversation after weeks of diapers and feeding. Instead, connecting with close friends who were going through a similar stage in their journey as working moms with young children proved to be a fantastic forum to share new experiences, ask tough questions, source emotional sustenance and practical advice.

Origin story

The idea for this book can be traced all the way back to that trip over the Bay Bridge. A friend named Ellen had dreamed up the idea of MOMSE, bringing together a circle of friends who were all new moms, but had met through their common commitment to tackling environmental sustainability issues through their work. Ellen saw that they could help each other get through the trials and tribulations of new motherhood while trying to foster sustainability in their own lives, much as they were attempting to do at work. For Lisa, being part of this group, sharing the joys and pains of life in a community of others going through a similar set of circumstances, was a revelation. This group was different even from conversations with other friends or moms she met at the playground and beyond what she could get from her husband, parents, work colleagues or her own self-reflection and education. The variety of perspectives and the validation that came from the group was empowering, and the purposeful focus on cultivating balance and sustainability, at home and at work, not just addressing the day-to-day challenges, was elevating.

When Lisa and her family moved to Washington, DC, two years later, she sorely missed being part of such a community of women with a common purpose. Fortunately, one of the first women she met down the street from her new home was Wendy, who invited her to join a neighborhood book club. As they got to know each other, Lisa explained the concept of MOMSE and they agreed on the spot to re-create MOMSE with a DC twist. On one of their first "walk and talks" on the trails of Woodley Park, they mapped out their plan and named the group Thrive.

Stronger together

For millennia, women have found value in getting together in groups to provide comfort, support and encouragement to one another. One of Wendy's favorite books, *The Red Tent*, imagines how, in biblical times, women used their monthly menstrual sequestration to build a common identity, community and resilience among the women of the tribe. Tupperware parties in the1950s, Consciousness Raising Groups in the 1970s, Microfinance Self-Help Groups in the 1990s and Lean in Circles in the 2010s are all structured ways that women come together to learn, laugh and support one another. Women's sports teams, women's groups at work, and girls' nights out are other ways we find to commune with our sisters.

Yet while these models exist, today we do not always reach for them as tools to thrive across all aspects of our lives. We may have been taught that we can be independent decision-makers or that only our husbands or our BFFs should be our confidantes and hear our greatest joys or our deepest concerns. We may suspect that other women are our competitors and be guarded around them. We may have friends we discuss kids with and friends we discuss work with, but never both. Or we may simply not have time or not be able to find a like-minded group of women or know how to build something that would serve our purposes.

What is new today is the level in which women are coming into their power, professionally, in their personal lives and in their communities. We believe that these networks can serve not just to comfort and instruct, but also to elevate and transform. This is best encapsulated by the soccer star Abby Wambach's brilliant coining of the phrase the "wolfpack." For Wambach, "there is a wolf inside of every woman. Her wolf is who she was made to be before the world told her who to be. Her wolf is her talent, her power, her dreams, her voice, her curiosity, her courage, her dignity, her choices—her truest identity." She then notes that "to bring out that wolf, every woman needs a Wolfpack. You really just need other women around you consistently, on an everyday basis going, 'No, we can do it differently. No, we can be better. No, you can do better.'"[57]

We have seen how the impact of groups like Thrive make us more resourceful, courageous, determined working women and help us find creative ways to push through. Monica works at the intersection of venture capital (VC), technology and financial industries, each of which are notoriously male dominated and often can be challenging for women. As the rare female, Latina VC fund manager in financial technology ("fintech"), Monica has had to examine and adapt industry norms – with respect to communication styles, networking approaches, incentive schemes and leadership models – to craft models that feel as authentic as they are effective. As the original co-founder of her fund, Quona Capital, Monica sought to build a more equitable and inclusive model of venture capital, but she faced pushback – sometimes in ways that delegitimized her perspective. Other Thrive women related similar experiences about constructive give-and-takes shifting to attacks. Or "mansplaining" that's especially common in more technical fields. Or having input discredited, only to later have them parroted by another colleague with greater credibility and confidence. A hilarious FedEx commercial called "Stolen Idea" hits home: around a conference table, one person's perfectly sound suggestion flops, only to be repeated by a well-coiffed man with assertive hand gestures, to universal praise.[58] The reality is that these commonly confronted situations can be maddening.

Unpacking, reframing and responding to these situations is exactly where a group like Thrive can be transformative. When Monica came to Thrive to process these subtle yet serious distinctions (e.g., between well-meaning feedback poorly delivered versus undermining commentary), her peers' insights, experience and honesty were invaluable. They helped her examine her assumptions and positions, consider the arguments, call her out if things might have been misconstrued, explore alternative narratives and motivations and shape a productive reaction where both finesse and forcefulness are needed. For example, removing any shaming or blaming in crafting responses can help the receiver digest and productively react and not be triggered by rebuttals.[59] Many Thrive women have worked in toxic environments or been gaslighted, and the ability to turn to a trusted circle to get wisdom and validation can help give us the tools and courage to persist – and lead differently.

We hear our own experience echoed when we listen to our sisters. It validates our instincts and gives us confidence in our own voices. We start connecting the dots and recognizing patterns, giving us insights and wisdom beyond what we would see alone. We troubleshoot our challenges through the lens of our shared values, enabling us to find new ways to solve problems. And we encourage and pledge our support and allegiance to one another giving us the resolve to take on the bigger challenges, and sometimes to fail.

The new girls club

Since high school, each of us has participated in many groups that have been instrumental in getting us through different stages of our lives, some personal like book clubs and playgroups, some professional like women's networks at work, and some both like Thrive. Though these groups come and go, they have all helped us build skills and networks that have enduring impacts on our lives.

Fresh out of business school, in the midst of the turn-of-the-century tech bubble, Monica, Wendy and some other friends created an investment club called Lakshmi Shares, named after the Hindu goddess of wealth. It was modeled after a similar initiative called "Just Economics" (an intentional double entendre) that Monica had been a part of in the Bay Area. Lakshmi Shares aimed to demystify complex topics and build skills and assets for the members. Though most of the women had Master's degrees in business or economics, they did not have deep experience managing money. Most of the women were starting careers in the impact investing and development finance space, so the group was a fun way to learn practical skills that helped them with both their personal and professional finance responsibilities.

Lakshmi Shares existed for several years, and more than the small profit and skills acquired, the women benefited from the lasting friendships they made. Over the years, they participated in each other's weddings, children's baptisms and mitzvahs, milestone birthdays, dinner parties, and more recently, Zoom cocktail hours. Moreover, as the women rose in their respective development finance and impact investing fields, these relationships became important professionally as well. What we did not expect at the time, but have come to appreciate, was that the "old boys club" that we have always envied and sometimes reviled is now available – in slightly different but as effective formats – to women through their own social networks. Because women tend to have deeper but less broad networks than men, it represents a tremendous asset for women as they build out these networks.

Indeed, 20 years after Lakshmi Shares shut its books, Monica, Wendy and two other former members found themselves in the Hague, as profiled speakers and participants in a series of events on global impact investing. They were respected leaders in their fields, drawing on skills they had honed, in part, over wine and spreadsheets many years before. They had cheered on and sometimes leaned on each other as they navigated their lives and careers, and the results were evident. After a celebratory dinner with a small crowd in honor of Monica's milestone birthday, the women found themselves sharing a nightcap and raising a toast to the enduring friendships and the legacy of Lakshmi Shares.

We got this

We all have friends and friend groups, and we sometimes come across ready-made groups, clubs or networks that welcome new members, and just like that we can join a community. But what if we want a more purposeful, or personalized, community of allies? Each of us has joined existing groups, but the experience of creating our own group with intentionality, like we did with Thrive, is uniquely fulfilling. We thought it might be helpful to share some of what we have learned running Thrive for the past decade.

Membership matters: The purpose of Thrive and the tone was set from the start with its clear membership criteria. All of the members have three things in common: they are moms who care deeply about helping their families to thrive, they have chosen a career in an impact field, and they are ambitious in terms of having increased impact through their work. The beauty of the selection criteria is that we have found like-minded women in similar stages of life who can support each other on their respective journeys. They have diverse sets of interests and professions from micro-finance to international development, and from corporate sustainability to entrepreneurship. However, a greater focus on member diversity would bring further perspectives to the group.

Making time: With a highly time-constrained group of women, finding time to connect can become an insurmountable challenge. Because Thrive is both a professional and personal network, we used the in-between spaces at work to make time. Our monthly luncheon reunions take us away from our offices at lunch hour. Our mini "flash" retreats have been scheduled from 3–8 p.m. to steal time from both work and home. And our walk-and-talks are on weekend mornings before the kids are up and/or soccer schedules kick off.

Prompt for purpose: The central purpose of Thrive is to help women find balance across their personal and professional lives. To stay true to this goal, each monthly conversation starts with a "check-in" that includes both a personal and professional update from each member. For most of us this is the only consistent forum we have to explore with equal depth and intensity both sides of our lives. The prompt gives equal standing to playground spats and boardroom negotiations and allows us to make connections between them that don't get made elsewhere. The wheel is a similar prompt that we use when we have more time to wade in, as we do during our periodic mini "flash" retreats.

Safe space: Thrive is a forum to listen empathetically and brainstorm creatively – as there are often parallels in each Thrive member's life. Thrive lunches are valuable to members because they are a safe space to talk about anything on their minds. We are comfortable bringing up tough things because we know that we will be listened to and not judged. We have consciously built a community where it feels good to put anything out on the table whether or not it puts us in a positive light, knowing that the other women are experiencing similar things, so have wells to draw upon in an empathetic way. Forgiveness to ourselves and each other is a common refrain as is how we support each other. We are very understanding of how stretched thin we all are and often laugh and commiserate about that instead of beating ourselves up over missing lunch or coming late. We're happy when we see each other and just jump right into the discussion in a frictionless way.

Operationalizing guiltlessness: We want participation in Thrive to always be a positive choice and we know priorities can shift. Therefore, at the start of each new school year we ask each member to opt in or out of Thrive for the next year. It is a choice without judgment. To opt in, members should expect to join for at least half of the lunches and at least one of the flash retreats. The benefit of the annual re-commitment is twofold. First, it allows for a continuous conversation to take place over the course of the year with some coming in and out but the majority carrying on from month to month. Second, it gives each woman the chance to be intentional about prioritizing the group against the dozens of other priorities she is juggling. Being able to take a hiatus or leave the group without guilt is just as important as maintaining the value for the women who stay in from year to year.

Keeping the energy alive: We've also noticed that behind every successful intentional community is one or two people ensuring the nuts and bolts are handled. In the case of Thrive, Lisa and Wendy's commitment to the group have been critical to nurturing the membership and evolving the group dynamics over a decade. Each play a different and complementary role. Lisa had the vision to create the group and puts in the effort monthly to ensure the logistics keep the group together. Wendy is an invaluable sounding board and partner to think through how to keep the group meaningful and growing to continue to meet the evolving needs of the women members. Without such champions, we have found groups run their course more quickly. Taking up that role enables us to spark a community that is bigger than ourselves and that can bring joy and support to many others.

What MOMSE, Lakshmi Shares and Thrive all have in common is that they were intentional communities created with a clear purpose known to all members. It's so easy with our busy lives being pulled in so many different directions daily to let things slide. One of the reasons that Thrive has persisted is that the conversations are deep and helpful. We share experiences from different vantage points and resources from across disciplines. We are as likely to discuss a Parental Encouragement Program (PEP)[60] technique as we are to exchange views on politics. We bring perspectives from our diverse backgrounds and learn from each other each time we come together. We've all been in groups that didn't feel quite right. The neighborhood book club that fizzled or the woman's network that never gelled. Finding the secret sauce requires some intentionality and iteration, but it is worth the effort.

Cultivating Communities that Reflect Our Values

It takes a village.
—Hillary Clinton

It was Wendy's turn to bring snacks for Naoma's preschool class. She rushed out of work, grabbed some snacks at Trader Joe's and made it to the class with a few minutes to spare. As she started to pre-sort the fruits and cookies into bowls, she listened in on the class. Sitting on the floor in intense conversation was a typically adorable group of 4-year-old kids. Wendy had gotten to know many of them and their parents. It constantly amazed her what a wildly diverse group of kids they were. Among them, half spoke Spanish at home, the other half English; several came from low-income households, while others were affluent. One's two dads, and the other's two moms had just acquired the legal right to wed; others lived with grandparents or single parents. Two had severe disabilities that kept them from walking or talking, while others were stunningly articulate. They represented a mini-UN of races and ethnicities.

That day, the teacher was leading a conversation about similarities and differences. In particular, how they were similar and different from each other. Wendy thought to herself, "Ooooh boy, this is going to be interesting." But as the kids' hands shot up, it was she that got schooled. A stunning African American girl compared her green eyes to her friend's blue eyes, more important in her mind than the fact that her friend had a rare illness that severely disabled him. Naoma mentioned that she was tall and her friend, whose two moms had just gotten married, was short. And a third boy whose immigrant parents spoke no English noted in a halting accent that he liked to play with blocks while his friend whose father worked at *The New*

York Times liked to draw. Wendy was stunned to realize that these children saw each other in a totally different way than she had been conditioned to see them. And she realized that it was not just the innocence of youth, but the intentional effort of the adults around them that encouraged their best instincts and helped them modulate the baser ones.

Most of the Thrive women grew up outside Washington, DC, and so were able to choose the neighborhoods, the schools and other communities we want to be a part of. That choice is powerful. Our values are reflected in the communities we choose, and in turn reflect back and get absorbed by us and our children. In this era of growing political and economic tribalism, the communities we choose say a lot about us. Wendy and Lisa both chose to settle in DC's Woodley Park neighborhood, and Monica in nearby Mount Pleasant when their children were young, in large part because of the vibrancy of the community, which, for families with young children, revolved around diverse and pioneering bilingual public schools. As Wendy saw on snack day, that bet paid off creating a deep vein of empathy and open mindedness that would stay with the children even as they moved to new schools and neighborhoods.

Intentional communities

So many points of light in our lives come from the communities we have chosen. Once we have children, and the local bar scene or flag football team is no longer a big social draw, most of our close personal connections come from our neighborhoods, the schools we attended and those we chose for our children, in addition to our workplaces, we have learned to bring the same intentionality in choosing and cultivating these communities, as we do to the other parts of our lives. The more we spend time and invest in those communities, the richer our lives are for it.

Woodley Park and Mount Pleasant turned out to be close-knit, friendly, and nurturing environments for families. A newcomer to Woodley Park described the community as "less like a neighborhood, more like a dorm" – with kids running from home to home and stimulating, hour-long front-porch conversations with neighbors. The neighborhood was just a block off of busy Connecticut Avenue and a ten-minute metro ride to downtown DC. The kids went to the neighborhood bilingual school where they were immersed in Spanish for half of each day. Kids and parents ran into each other playing with chalk on the sidewalks, walking to school, or climbing trees on the grounds of a nearby hotel. Most parents – moms and dads had interesting careers, and sidewalk conversations were as likely to be about bitcoin as babysitters. The postage-stamp sized front yards became a communal easter-egg hunt on Easter, and a riot of candy and costumes on Halloween, not to mention the moon bounces and water slides at the summer block party they organized. There are neighborhoods like this everywhere, of every socio-economic status, the key is to seek them out as they can help to shape our families in so many ways.

When we have young children, there are endless hours of playdates, trick-or-treating in the neighborhood and camping trips. While the kids play, the friendships we develop with the other parents who happen to be there can be enduring. Having as a starting point a community with shared values makes it more likely we'll find our people. Wendy remembers chatting with the other moms on her son's first day at the neighborhood school, thinking, "Wow, I really, really hope our boys become friends, so that I can hang out with these kick-ass women!" In fact, those "kick-ass" women she met in the hallway that day did become some of her best friends. Over time, even as their sons moved to different schools and pursued different interests, the friendships evolved and deepened. Ten years after meeting in the hallway, one of the moms led a service trip to South Africa to explore inequality there compared to the US, and her son and Tibor went along. The mothers marched and volunteered together for the causes that were important to them. And when COVID-19 came along, they came together over a front-yard fire pit, sometimes to despair, sometimes to celebrate and always to compare notes about life: how we're managing with aging parents, what is pandemic-normal for home-bound teenagers, or just how exactly Tik Tok works.

Indeed, these "intentional communities" or "urban tribes" have taken on greater import in an era (even pre-COVID-19) where technology allowed us to work remotely and economic forces accelerated autonomous work structures.[61] More of us are part of dual working couples which means greater dependence on neighbors to figure out homework assignments, pick kids up from school and activities, and just keep an eye out that they're safe. In many ways, choosing where we live is a choice about who is also raising our kids – the schools they attend, the kids they play with, the parents who chaperone them. Our neighbors play the role our extended families used to, when we lived closer together.

The power of community had become clear to Wendy some years before as she was preparing to head home from work one day. Since Max was at a conference in New York, she would have to pick up her son Tibor from pre-school and make it home in time to relieve their nanny who was taking care of their one-year-old twins, Ava and Naoma. As Wendy was getting ready to leave work, she got a panicked call from her nanny that there had been a freak accident and part of Ava's finger had been sliced off. Wendy dropped everything and ran for a taxi. In the ten minutes it took her to get home, here's what happened: she called her neighbor from the taxi, who ran across the street and got another neighbor, a pediatrician, to come and help Ava. Another doctor from two doors down and a half dozen other neighbors were standing by ready to help. Wendy's work colleague had run to the pre-school to bring Tibor home, another neighbor was calming and debriefing the nanny, in Spanish. By the time the fire engine, ambulance and Wendy all converged at their home, Ava was already bandaged up and ready to go to the hospital. Wendy will never forget being met with a calm baby and the cluster of caring faces, instead of the messy agony that she was expecting. It was truly astonishing. As Wendy jumped in the ambulance with Ava, she knew Naoma and Tibor would be in good hands with the entire community pitching in. At the hospital, they were able to sew Ava's well bandaged finger back on with no long-term damage. No less miraculous was how the event further knit together their little community.

Time well spent

No community, school or neighborhood is perfect and when we choose one, we need to think about how we show up in the face of those imperfections. Very soon after becoming a parent there seems to be an unlimited number of requests to pitch in: for school fundraising campaigns, school committees, and as class parents. Our neighborhoods need us too, to weigh in on a zoning dispute or redistricting measure. When we do engage, it can give us some of our most fulfilling experiences or it can leave us feeling like we've wasted our time.

As working parents, our binding constraint is time. We have all volunteered for what seemed like a good cause only to sit through endless debates about minutiae or be given volunteer tasks that seemed nearly meaningless, and wondered "how did I get here, and how soon can I leave?" It is worth being rigorous in assessing how an opportunity can benefit from a specific skill set we have, and whether we are passionate enough about it to devote the time it requires. Working in a tech company, Lisa saw a curricular gap in tech skills at her daughter's public elementary school. Inspired to close this skills gap and upgrade the hardware available to the students, Lisa helped raise a "Tech for Tigers" fund as part of the annual school auction and launched coding programs at the school. It soon became a family affair as her daughter's girl scout troop ran tech support and the kids learned to code.

Volunteering can be the ultimate multitasking activity, combining doing good with deepening relations with the people we are doing them with. We have forged some of our deepest friendships on field trips to pumpkin patches and have rekindled old friendships canvassing together for political campaigns. As children get older and can volunteer at neighborhood food drives, march at protests, or participate in clothing drives, it can be incredibly satisfying to work together to help build the community fabric. It gives us a chance to see our child learning and developing new perspectives. It also helps our children see us in a fresh context, deepening appreciation and creating new bonds, especially valuable as they get to the trickier adolescent ages.

Tough choices

Sometimes, in spite of our hopes and efforts, it is time to move on. Families outgrow houses, schools become inadequate for children's needs, and needs and priorities shift. The decision to move can be an agonizing one with many trade-offs, but it is another part of our journey, and another opportunity for us to "create our own adventure."

Monica had purchased her first home in Mount Pleasant because it had all the elements she sought in a community – a real sense of neighborhood with its farmers' market and quirky retail strip; diverse demographics with a colorful mix of Latinos, return Peace Corps volunteers and upwardly mobile progressives; and access to nature through the adjacent Rock Creek Park. Mt. Pleasant is where she met her husband and where her kids were born, so they invested a lot in trying to make it their home. But eventually their family outgrew their house. At the same time, the public school was struggling, in spite of active involvement from Monica, her spouse and friends. The public versus private school decision became a focal point of their discussions on what would come next, a discussion charged because each had been raised with different experiences. Monica and Jordan focused on what was important for their children: Could they walk to school? Were there safe places to play outside? Were there too many privileged displays of wealth? Was there diversity? Were parents involved in the school? There were trade-offs, but weighing these factors influenced their choice to move three miles north to a tight-knit community just over the Maryland border. What attracted them to their new neighborhood was the strong public schools, the bike trails and public spaces, including a park adjacent to their house, and the concentration of friends that shared their values and vision for the kind of connected community they wanted to create.

Living abroad: gratitude for privilege

Monica and Jordan were happy in their new village, though they had to make a conscious choice to forgo urban living and the racial and ethnic diversity of their old neighborhood. Monica shared these concerns with other Thrive members making similar moves, who wanted to figure out how to keep exposing their kids to the aspects less evident in the communities they chose to call home. She was inspired by Lisa and her husband's carpe diem decision to temporarily relocate to the Spanish Basque Country for six months and to spend long summers there in her husband's hometown where they could raise their daughter bilingually and close to her Spanish family and roots. After living abroad with her own family at age four, Lisa knew first-hand how early experiences can open up perspectives on alternate realities from an early age.

Monica and her husband also wanted their kids to understand their privilege, to understand the world from a lens outside of the United States, and to appreciate the liberties and opportunities this country offers. After 10 years of balancing parenting with international investing, Monica was also eager to be closer to the portfolio companies she managed, half of which were in South Africa, and have the family share in a life-abroad experience while the kids were still in grade school. Monica fixated on the idea of bringing her family to South Africa – to share the excitement she had felt when she had moved there after business school, leaving the Silicon Valley at the peak of the internet boom in the late '90s pulled by the vision of the post-apartheid rainbow nation led by Nelson Mandela. The family read up on the country's history and natural wonders, and when the time came, limited their haul to the airlines' checked bag maximums to travel light.

The year-long trip made a big impact on the Engels – each individually and as a family unit. The kids learned about the complicated history of one of Africa's most developed economies and the power of Truth and Reconciliation. They also learned lessons about grit and managing in a new environment where they didn't have friends and didn't share some of the languages and customs. They adapted and spent time outdoors, learning new skills (cricket and juggling) and building confidence. Monica got a lesson in operating in a culture that puts a premium on downtime – spending weekends hiking or day tripping rather than schlepping to soccer games (which were held after school) or working. And Jordan was able to pursue some of his professional passions – aerial photography and finding social entrepreneurs to mentor. They lived very contently in a home that was a fraction of the square footage of the one back home, with a manual transmission rental that did the job without a fuss, and without any of the "things" that seem so necessary to have – from kitchen appliances to the right shoes for different occasions. Living with less at home made them orient outwards to the stunning natural settings and outdoor lifestyle (they lived within hiking distance of famed Table Mountain and Lion's

Head). Most importantly, the time, health-oriented environment and balance made them reflect deeply on their privilege and how they could return home with more empathy and a stronger commitment to bridging divides – economically, politically and culturally.

Normalizing breaks: time outs and perspective changes

Though the time abroad was magical, Monica's family was eager to get home. They missed their family and close friends, and the warm comfort of one's home. They came back to a very polarized country – with political fault lines more clearly visible and an increase in volume that was jarring. These divisions were even visible within their community havens – as social media and news feeds tailored their messages to form echo chambers, even between neighbors. The Thrive women discussed these troubling trends, exchanging notes on how to raise kids in a way that exposed them to these debates while teaching them active listening skills and empathy.[62] And they noted the arguments that surfaced among friends – and even within families – regardless.

For Monica and her family, these tensions reached a boiling point in the first peak of the COVID-19 pandemic and the Black Lives Matter protest. Fueled also by COVID-19 claustrophobia, the Engel family planned an RV trip to both spend time in this country's inspiring natural beauty and with people whose lived experience and worldview was very different than that of those in their Chevy Chase community. The trip did not disappoint on either front. They covered over seven thousand miles in four weeks and reinforced a belief that was popular among Thrive women: what people (even from diverse backgrounds and life experiences) have in common is much more powerful than what differentiates them.

Lisa's family also "chose their own adventure" during the COVID-19 pandemic. Relocating to South Florida, they enjoyed resetting in a place with ties to her husband's Spanish-speaking heritage and living with neighbors open to discussing multiple viewpoints and perspectives. While it can be comfortable in our increasingly homogenous ideological bubbles, they found it refreshing to be in a place that had a greater diversity of views and openness to discussing them dispassionately, or not at all, something that could be difficult to find in DC with its strong one-party bent. Being thrust into environments that were politically and economically diverse taught Monica, Lisa and their families an important lesson.

Where we choose to settle, and where we choose to journey is an important part of our life path and shapes the way we and our families situate ourselves in the world. We should not underestimate how our neighborhoods, schools, communities shape us and support us. They are part of the scaffolding that lets us be who we are and will affect the people our children become. The more we find ways to root ourselves in supportive communities, while finding ways to branch out to the broader world, the better citizens of the world we and our families will be.

Being the Change We Want to See

If we only accept what we can see, we will never change anything. If we don't go to our imagination, we will only get what we've always gotten.
—Glennon Doyle

When Lisa and her husband started to think about having kids in 2006 – the year that the *Inconvenient Truth* came out – something that kept her up at night was figuring out how to remove toxins from their life to prepare their home for a newborn. Not knowing where to start, she asked a friend who ran a San Francisco based NGO called Net Impact for advice. A fellow MOMSE member, her friend gave Lisa some basic tips about swapping out cleaning products. Thinking even bigger, she also invited her to join the just launched Net Impact Green Challenge. A three-month competition to see how far corporate volunteer teams could move their company's environmental agenda forward. Intrigued, Lisa reached out to the dozen or so Net Impact members at her company. She was inspired to see a rapid response from colleagues in just a few hours. The next thing she knew, the group had mobilized over seventy-five volunteers, secured sponsors, and developed a plan to measure and reduce the company's environmental impact in the US. When her team won first prize in the competition, she started to field inbound inquiries from other companies about how to apply their lessons learned. Keen to build on the green thread, she translated the interest into a new job for herself building a sales pipeline for sustainability projects and creating a green team. This was one of many examples of Thrive women taking a personal interest in tackling a societal challenge and finding a way to turn it into a professional pursuit.

The urge to "repair the world"

In our work and in our lives, we have agency not just to design a life that we love, but to pay it forward and make a better world for others. Something that all Thrive members share, by design, is that there is a strong social impact component to our work. That is not an especially distinguishing factor for professional women in DC, but it is an important part of our identity as a group and as individuals. Our day jobs are to help make the world a better place, find solutions that will improve lives, and advocate for change.

Much of what we see that needs to change, whether at work or in our communities, is beyond our formal job descriptions. But this rarely stops us. We see corporate cultures that keep women and minorities from thriving. We see systematic inequalities that thwart the potential of individuals, communities and economies. We see a civic culture that is increasingly tribal and polarized. We see a world that is ecologically out of balance. 2020 in particular drove home the extent of our nation's fault lines, in healthcare, income and racial inequality, political divides, the climate crisis and mental health.

These are monumental challenges that require all of us to do our part. As professionals who have been able to effect change, we know we have skills, resources, and accrued privileges that we can put to good use for the causes we care about. We are not satisfied with the status quo. And yet, it is not always clear how to have a real, lasting impact on such complex and intransigent challenges. We wonder if it is our place to get involved in issues that we don't fully understand. We see that making a dent requires conviction and courage to confront entrenched views. We recognize that our privilege may get in the way. It can be tempting just to do the job we are paid to do, do it well, and leave it at that.

Outside our swim lane

When we overcome our misgivings, we realize that though

we can't do it all, we can find ways to make a difference. Of course, we can contribute our time, our energy, our knowledge and money to the causes we care about. But, the most powerful tool we often have is our voice and our example. Often, we can have the biggest impact with simple words and actions that take courage and conviction. As a role model, an influencer, an advocate and an ally we can contribute to meaningful change if we have the courage of our convictions.

Monica didn't know what to think when a young rising star in her team took her aside and told her, almost in tears, that she was pregnant. Though it should have been a joyful moment, the anxiety in her colleague's voice was unmistakable. After congratulating her on the news, Monica gently inquired why she sounded so shaky. The colleague explained that she wasn't sure how she would be able to manage in an organizational culture and industry that demanded speed, agility and dedication, sometimes at the expense of all else. The admission triggered a flood of familiar thoughts and feelings for Monica – many years of difficult decisions and missed moments of her own, and hours of panel discussions unpacking why a fast-paced industry like venture capital was so unforgiving for women and what could be done about it.

Though the experience and emotions were familiar, Monica had to admit that there was neither a playbook nor easy answers. She wasn't even sure if she could claim to be a great role model. She always struggled with following her own advice: focusing on doing a few things extraordinarily, letting other things go, communicating and collaborating, prioritizing refueling. What she could say to her colleague with confidence, was that she and her partners were committed to building an inclusive organization. They wanted their staff – mothers and fathers alike – to grow professionally, thrive personally and find parenting paradigms they felt good about. They knew there would be trade-offs. The year before, they had cataloged the creative ways their fund and its portfolio companies were fostering inclusive work environments that enabled people with diverse backgrounds and needs to thrive.[63] By examining and sharing these approaches, they hoped to raise awareness and spur actions that would enable this colleague, and others like her, to better balance their personal needs with that of their demanding workplace. Monica and her partners were committed to making Quona work for their investment colleagues as they started families, lest their fund, their investees and the industry lose out on a phenomenal pool of talent.

Being the change we want to see means not just staying in our most comfortable swim lane, but using our assets – both positional power and soft influence, to go beyond. We all know women who lead by example but do nothing to make it easier – or at least less treacherous – for others to follow. By virtue of her position, many consider Monica a role model for women in the venture capital and fintech industries. But it is her effort to tackle diversity and inclusion issues within her portfolio where she goes beyond. She had to expend professional capital to have difficult conversations with men and women, who did not necessarily see the lack of women or minorities in their midst as an issue. She had to make herself vulnerable in being transparent about her family obligations in order to destigmatize that conversation at work. And she had to be a proactive ally of those team members that were trying to find greater balance, even if there was a risk that they would not succeed.

Though still a work in progress, she knows she has already made her mark, generating awareness among her colleagues, seeding new ideas with her fund and its portfolio companies, influencing the dialogue in her industry, and giving hope to the young investment associates who need to be told they, too, will be able to manage it.

Wake-up call

Supporting women at work has long been an important cause for each of us, but the COVID-19 crisis compelled us to look more broadly at the inequalities in our communities, especially when it came to healthcare, income and education. Our relatively comfortable quarantine arrangements were so starkly different from the experience of so many others, leading many of us to search for ways that we could make a difference.

For Lisa, the realization hit the morning after the government shuttered schools where she lived. She woke up before dawn wondering how going virtual would affect public school kids. So many depend on schools, community centers and libraries for breakfast and lunch, access to computers and printers, and before and after-school care. She had an idea. What if she could mobilize a network of experts on digital connectivity and learning to help local leaders close the digital divide for those students unable to get online? In a matter of days, a team was assembled and rolling up sleeves. She was motivated to work faster seeing how hard it was for her own daughter to transition to virtual school even with all the access to technology she needed and parents at home who could support.

These efforts were just one example of the type of projects her colleagues mobilized early in the COVID-19 crisis with social innovators around the world connecting students, patients, entrepreneurs and NGOs to food, healthcare, learning, small business loans, and other critical services. She was blown away by how teams courageously dove in to do whatever they could to improve a very difficult situation and overcoming difficulties in their own lives during the pandemic to serve others. The experience reinforced an important lesson about the power of unlocking the unbeatable combination of human creativity and drive coupled with networks and resources to tackle problems bigger than any one of us.

When we look at challenges so much bigger than ourselves,

we have found we can often do more by leveraging whatever assets we can get our hands on. It may be the organizations that we work in. It may be the neighbors on our community listserv. Or it may be our skills that make the difference.

Another Thrive woman found herself overcome by stories of children at the border being separated from their parents and felt compelled to help. She sent donations and asked others to do the same. But it didn't feel like it was enough. As a lawyer, she understood the legal morass these families were wading into and knew that they would not be able to navigate it on their own. She realized she could give more than money, and that with her skills she could be a voice to advocate for them. So, she took time off work, signed up as a volunteer and traveled to Texas to defend the rights of immigrants that had been questionably detained and separated from their children. The work was emotionally draining but also invigorating. Coming home, she found she could not imagine setting it aside, and parlayed her passion and her skill set into a new job focused on protecting the rights and wellbeing of immigrant communities around the world.

Waste not, want not

2020 was a terrible year by any account: half a million deaths from the pandemic, historic economic and jobs losses, democracy under fire, a racial reckoning. On top of all of these metaphorical fires burning, there were also record-setting fires that engulfed California and Australia, locusts that swarmed India and Africa, and huge damage done by cyclones, hurricanes and other natural disasters around the globe.

For those of us who are not experts in carbon taxes, electric car batteries or reforestation, the climate challenges seems so big and our ability to make a difference so small. When Wendy looked at her own carbon footprint, she felt more helpless than empowered. Her job required her to travel, their house and cars were not due for upgrades, and with a family of five the volume of waste they created was impressive. One day, her daughter Ava showed her a TED Talk by Bea Johnson,[64] touting a zero-waste lifestyle. The talk convincingly argued that incremental measures were not enough. She suggested a more intentional approach to reducing, reusing and recycling, with the goal of *zero* household waste. She gave practical ideas about how to redesign purchasing and consumption habits that actually seemed do-able. Wendy and Ava decided to make a project of it and focus on the kitchen. Over the course of a year, they revamped their purchasing and food storage habits, expanded their composting and ramped up recycling, significantly reducing what their family wasted and sent to landfills.

The work came naturally to Wendy. For the most part, she did the grocery shopping, managed the leftovers and compost, and policed the recycling. What took it beyond, was seeing the small ripple effects that her efforts were having. Ava was becoming a passionate advocate of waste-reduction and gave a presentation at school. Fellow shoppers noticed the reusable produce bags and lack of plastics in her shopping basket and got curious. Grocers and restaurants got comfortable putting deli meats or take-out foods into the reusable tins she brought with her. It wasn't always easy, and it could be awkward, but she felt like she was changing minds in her own small way.

Perhaps most consequentially, over lunch one day, Wendy shared her zero-waste journey with a friend (and Lakshmi Shares alum) Stephanie Miller, who was passionate about the concept herself. The two of them compared notes and sparked interest among their friends. Taking it to the next level, Stephanie wrote a book, *Zero-Waste Living the 80/20 Way*[65] and now advocates and consults through her business ZeroWasteinDC.com. Stephanie's goal with her new business is to help busy people make necessary changes that will have a ripple effect that could lead to systemic change. And so it goes. The ripples are getting larger, totally beyond Ava and Wendy's initial spark.

We all have opportunities like this, to inform and inspire others to make changes that will have ripple effects beyond ourselves and our families. Sometimes it doesn't take a lot of effort, but it may trigger meaningful change. Over time, these ripple effects can help create the change we want to see on a much greater scale.

Conclusion

We set out to write this book at the beginning of the COVID-19 pandemic and completed it as the light at the end of the tunnel is getting closer. COVID-19 has had a profound impact on all of our lives. It shook us to the core as we watched decades of progress on critical issues such as poverty alleviation, academic advancement, and economic gains vaporize with prolonged shutdowns. COVID-19 also had a particularly severe impact on women. Millions paused or abandoned careers to take on teaching their kids thrust into virtual school without proper training. Moms and dads stepped up to fill in gaping holes that many local governments and school districts could not. It also widened the fault lines between the "knowledge economy" and those who cannot work remotely.

COVID-19 forced us to stop, take stock, and redefine how we show up at work, at home and in our communities. It grounded us from traveling, forced more simplicity in our daily lives, brought us back to basics, and called us to reprioritize what's most important to us and to our families. It has brought us full circle to re-evaluate our lives, like the wheel that has inspired Thrive conversations for the last decade. It is time to define what the new normal looks like in a way that builds back better – not just for us, but for all women and men that seek to intentionally create more balance across all dimensions of their lives: work, family, self and community.

On the work front, we have felt called to recommit to our careers with social purpose as COVID-19 has laid bare and widened the fissures in our society between the privileged and the disenfranchised. We have been awed by the talented pioneers across sectors and countries who were able to invent, produce and distribute new types of vaccines mobilizing public and private sector resources in innovative ways and at unprecedented speed. We see a new model of leadership emerging, covered with women's fingerprints and turbocharged by a workplace that empowers women to thrive, where women are empowered to ascend the three levels of the leadership ladder. We see this starting with mastering one's own trade, building confidence in oneself and others and clarifying boundaries. As we move on to becoming managers that listen, elevate, empower, create stability and safety in our work environments we can influence others and create positive change. When we are able to build coalitions, reframe narratives; overcome toxic mindsets and behaviors; shape organizational culture and accelerate the drive for greater impact, we can influence systems far beyond our direct domain.

On the family front, COVID-19 has shined a bright spotlight on the role of mothers in families. As the husband of one Thrive member put it: "You are the backbone of this family; if you are not well, none of us will be." Yet we need to explore new ways to define expectations, roles and responsibilities, and to reduce the guilt we too often feel. To do so requires scaffolding at work and at home, the support structures that can flex to accommodate individual needs. Also, we need to step back and let our partners and kids take the ball and run with it – and find their own paths. As we do, we see how time and mindshare become available to communicate the unspoken, appreciate the small gestures, share more clearly our needs and preferences and find ways to articulate our families' core values. In these unencumbered moments we build precious memories and long-lasting connections – the mortar that holds the bricks of the family foundation together.

Personally, we have given ourselves permission to draw boundaries, to self-care, refuel and celebrate. Thrive women are listening more to our intuition, focusing more on pacing and tending to our own oxygen masks to enable us to better help those around us. Maintaining healthy habits – diet, exercise, sleep, recharge – becomes a joyful quest rather than a source of guilt. We have encouraged each other to reframe the narrative around the frustrations we sometimes feel and to laugh! The reminder to celebrate starts small with daily gratitude about how fortunate we are, taking stock of our health, friendships, professional opportunities and livelihood. We also encourage each other to carve out time to celebrate – milestone birthdays and work accomplishments as well as smaller wins.

In our communities, we have seen how important it is to be intentional about picking and contributing to the neighborhoods, schools and communities that help us raise our families. They reinforce the values and create the conditions necessary to have thriving family and work lives. Though communities change constantly, those that foster strong values of respect, contribution, pay-it-forward, diversity and empathy are truly gifts that keep giving. We also see the powerful role that women as mothers, leaders and advocates can have when we engage with intentionality and focus, whether in the PTA, in a state referendum, a national election or a global engagement. Similarly, and closer to home, we have built wolfpacks to support each other and interweave these groups to build a strong, cultural fabric that both fortifies and centers them.

Across these core life elements are some recurring themes and insights as to how we move forward, intentionally, to redefine a new normal:

Boundaries: Time and again, we have seen the transformative effect when working mothers and fathers draw effective boundaries on their own working hours, family time, and time to refuel — and then give themselves and their colleagues permission to honor these fine lines. We accept that we cannot be devoted to all parts of our wheels at once. Sometimes, good is "good enough." There are times in life when we need to deprioritize an important part of our wheel because another part needs us more, such as when we have small children and our balance of time outside work may shift more inside the home than outside. This is a call to be more intentional in finding what works for us at different stages of our lives and forgiving ourselves when we fall short. Balance cannot always be pursued on a daily or even weekly basis. There are times we will be busy at work or with family commitments and neglect our morning meditation, and that's okay, for a period of time. Our career, our marriages and child raising are all marathons – not sprints. We cannot operate at 100% all the time on all fronts and must resist the pressure to continually perform, please, perfect. Rather than let unfulfilled expectations get the best of us, we focus on bringing our best to whatever we're doing at the time – whether working, parenting, or self-caring.

Networks & wolfpacks: It is critical to cultivate a community of relationships – with our spouses, neighbors, extended family, coworkers, friends and others. These networks are both the social capital and safety net we need to fully tap our strengths. As women, our networks can be dazzlingly multifaceted and abysmally under-valued. Our children may teach us our greatest leadership lessons, our colleagues may have the key to bedtime struggles, our fellow school chaperone may unlock a key partnership opportunity, and our friend can help us sort it all out with grace. Finding ways to nurture and build our networks is essential. Our networks are a largely untapped superpower that enrich every aspect of our lives and can grow and evolve as we do.

Listening: All facets of our lives are improved when we take the time to truly listen to ourselves and to others. So many women have forged paths that we gratefully walk upon and whose voices and experiences resonate within us. When we are still and can actively listen to, rather than quiet, these voices, we can tap that collective wisdom and strengthen our own intuition of what, deep down, we know is right. When we do, we discover strength, resilience and courage that can help us with the ebb and flow of our own journey. No less important is to actively listen to others, whether it is our children, our bosses or that crazy neighbor. Active listening involves not just listening but reflecting on our own inner narratives, like "my boss is threatened by me" or "my partner doesn't appreciate me" and questioning them. We sometimes walk around with great certainty that we know what our co-workers or family members are thinking, but, what if we're wrong? Listening better frees us to inquire, test assumptions, and build a richer reality rooted in intuition and understanding.

Agency: Each of us has agency, the ability to find ways to shape our lives and the world around us in line with our true north. While the scope of this agency is heavily prescribed by socio-economic factors, even in small doses it can be powerful. Well before we have any formal power, we can ask questions, make requests, and take the initiative. By getting clear on our non-negotiables, clarifying boundaries, finding allies who share our beliefs and identifying productive ways to have our voices heard, we can change the world around us for the better. This extends to our belief that by working together, we can make a difference, whether to achieve the UN Sustainable Development Goals in the "decade to deliver" or improve our local schools.

Voice: We value our ability to challenge long-held assumptions, to make requests, to speak the unspoken with conviction and confidence. We have strength and powers that may not have been fully leveraged in a system designed for a different reality, i.e., one stay at home parent versus two working spouses; jobs for life versus regular job switching; highly structured organizations versus the gig economy. We encourage women and men to find communities of support – at home and at work – to provide sounding boards, solidarity and solace knowing the journey ahead can be as rewarding as it is hard if forged together.

We hope this book inspires others to form groups, expand

their networks, find their voice, chart new paths, build new bridges, and rebalance. We have been encouraged by the amazing strides so many women have taken before us; and have included resources in this book that we hope will help others on their journey. It is so exciting to see the ways in which the world is becoming more reflective of women's lives, their needs and their perspectives. But we still see so many opportunities for improvement, where the powerful voices of women are needed more than ever. We are excited to watch women, especially younger women, continue to shape the rules of the game and express their voices in authentic and bold ways. We look forward to continuing the conversation and the journey to thrive.

In gratitude

As we wrote this book, we often reflected on how lucky we were to have the resources, relationships and jobs that have enabled us to weather the COVID-19 pandemic with relative ease. As millions of mothers left the workforce facing impossible choices between being caregivers, teachers and breadwinners, we were imbued with a deep sense of gratitude for the choices that we had. We watched with dismay as the pandemic was devastating for so many. We will always be immensely grateful that when the crisis hit, we were working in organizations that we believed in and that could go virtual overnight, with supportive partners who were right there problem solving with us every day, living in homes with jobs that could comfortably sustain us, and with children who were old enough to learn and grow through virtual or hybrid schooling without requiring our minute-to-minute attention.

So many factors contributed to our being able to thrive through COVID-19 with the time, space and wherewithal to do our work, be good parents, spouses, daughters, sisters, and citizens and still have time to write. Among them are countless women and men who have inspired us throughout the nearly two years we spent creating this book, the decade of Thrive, and a lifetime of role models and experiences. It would be impossible to name all of those whose ideas, experiences, passions, stories have informed this book, but a few must be highlighted.

Warren Buffet said the best career decision you can make is who you marry, and we could not agree more. During COVID-19, there were weeks and even months when the only adult conversation that was not virtual was with our respective spouses, Jordan, Álvaro and Max. We became even more aware of how lucky we were to have husbands who supported us and shared in our burdens and our joys equally. As we worked on this book, our husbands believed in us, shared their own insights and perspectives, and – the greatest gift of all – graciously gave us the space we needed to create as we disappeared every Sunday morning for a year. They even had some great suggestions for the book's title, like: "WTF: Women Thrive Forward," "Thriving our Way," or "Ballsy Guide to Kicking A** in a Post COVID World." Though they didn't make it to the front cover, we are boundlessly grateful for their love, levity and support.

Our children, Sophie, Isaac, Bella, Tibor, Ava and Naoma, are perhaps our greatest source of inspiration in our writing and in our lives. Through the lockdowns, we have been privileged to watch up close as they emerged through their teenage years into the people they will become. We have been awed by their aptitude, resilience, and unique perspectives on life. Particularly during COVID-19, they have been equal parts our companions and sparring partners, our students and teachers, our fresh pair of eyes and our anchors.

Our parents gave us our spirit, our fortitude and our confidence to go forth, find our voices and make a difference in this world and have our eternal love and gratitude. Our siblings, aunts, cousins, mentors, friends and colleagues around the world have likewise helped shape us into the women we are today and the core values that come through in this book. They are too numerous to name, but they should know how grateful we are to have them in our lives and for their contributions, big and small to this book.

The seeds of this book were planted in a decade of conversations with fellow Thrive members in Washington, DC, including Fiona Macaulay, Katherine McQuaid, Melissa Johns, Melissa Ingber, Greta Bull, Momina Aijazuddin, Belinda Cherrington, Veronica Sanchez, Jennifer Staats, Victoria White, Kristin Sharp, Denise Naguib, Allison Butler, Kelly Cronin, Rosario Londono, Gretchen Zucker, Amanda Ripley, and Sarah Prosser. The idea for Thrive germinated in conversations the decade prior in the Bay Area with members of MOMSE including Ellen Weinreb, Sara Ellis Conant, and Liz Maw. We have done our best to channel these dear friends' stories, wisdom, and inspiration though we do not always identify them by name. Thank you for being with us through the highs and the lows of the past two decades and for having the courage to hold up a mirror to us when we needed one.

We have many more people to thank for helping us get this labor of love over the finish line, including the very talented graphic designer Kica Worrilow for generously designing the wheel illustration. A big shout out to the wonderfully patient publishing team at Changemakers Books led by Tim Ward who helped us through all of the twists and turns, always believing that the "snow leopards" would come through in the end. Thanks to all those from around the world who encouraged us with comments and advice on the manuscript at different stages from idea all the way through to publication including Shannon Austin, Angela Bekkers, Nici Butchart, Lauren Cochran, Nancy Cordes, Jacquelyn Davis, Lyndsay Holley Handler, Jamie Horwitz, Maggie Lake, Anne-Gaëlle Le Vaillant, Christina Ling, Ann Mehl, Stephanie Miller, Carol Neuberger, Ioana Popescu, Abby Russell, Sara Taylor and Hillary Miller Wise.

Finally, we were lucky to have each other to lean on as friends and allies as we navigated the pandemic, a transformational prior decade, and, in Monica's and Wendy's case, a shared journey since grad school. We were there to support each other as we explored the white spaces and the gray spaces; to commiserate and be sounding boards when we felt lost or confused; and, to celebrate the good times. Many of the lessons of this book first came from stories, experiences, articles, podcasts or books that we felt compelled to share with each other on walk and talks, late nights, and stolen moments in our search for meaning and hacks to make our lives both fuller and easier. Indeed, one of the advantages of writing this book together was that with three perspectives on every topic, we were able to unlock our deeper, collective wisdom even as we each personally are still finding our own way. This is the promise of friendship fulfilled, to have a communion that makes each of us greater than the sum of our parts.

About the authors

Monica Brand Engel is a wife, mother of twins, as well as an investor, entrepreneur, and co-founding Managing Partner of Quona Capital. She has launched funds and products aimed at broadening financial inclusion globally. Monica spent her formative years in Silicon Valley, building alternative financing companies targeted at near-bankable businesses and earning dual degrees at Stanford's Graduate School of Business and Graduate School of Education. Longing to apply lessons learned in emerging markets, she moved to South Africa after graduating Stanford, to work in venture capital (with Anthuri) in a nascent ecosystem. From Cape Town, she was recruited by Accion as Head of Product + Innovation, to launch new financial services to underserved businesses and consumers globally – including an extended stint in Mexico with Compartamos, re-branded Gentera Bank following its IPO in 2007. This IPO provided the funds and the mandate to launch Accion's Frontier Investments – its first fintech for inclusion fund and the predecessor to Quona Capital. Monica loves travel, dinner parties, and dancing and finds balance doing yoga, spending time in nature and exploring with her family.

Lisa Neuberger Fernandez is a wife, mom of a teen and a puppy, visionary social innovator, sustainability strategist, and Unusual Pioneer recognized by Yunus Social Business and the Schwab Foundation for Social Entrepreneurship. As a Managing Director at Accenture, she led global strategy and innovation teams to up-skill and empower social innovators in fifty countries to have a net positive impact on society. In her over twenty-four years at Accenture, Lisa and her teams founded and ran highly innovative cross-sector collaborations to create a more sustainable future such as the Sustainability Innovation Challenge, Social Innovators Accelerator, Public Service Value, and NGO consulting spin-off New Sector Alliance. A thought leader, speaker and patent holder, Lisa co-authored the *Social Innovators Guidebook, Inclusive Future of Work: A Call to Action,* and *New Skills Now.* She has lived and worked abroad in France and Spain and graduated with dual master degrees from the Wharton School of Business and the Fletcher School of Law and Diplomacy. She is a great connector who loves to learn and finds balance walking on the beach with family and friends, singing jazz, and playing tennis.

Wendy Jagerson Teleki is a wife, mother of three teens, and daughter of entrepreneurs, who has spent her career spearheading efforts to help private and public institutions in emerging markets expand financing and support for small businesses and women entrepreneurs. With the International Finance Corporation, she led programs to privatize and build the small business sector in Ukraine in the early 1990s, developed solutions for SMEs in Indonesia during the Asian Financial Crisis, launched innovative SME finance and advisory offerings and pioneered blended finance efforts. Currently, she heads the secretariat of the Women Entrepreneurs Finance Initiative (We-Fi) housed in the World Bank, which aims to break down barriers and increase financing for women entrepreneurs in over

60 developing countries around the world. She is the editor of the *Last Leather Helmets*, an extraordinary tale of an everyman in extraordinary times. She has an MA in International Economics from Johns Hopkins School of Advanced International Studies (SAIS) and an MBA in Finance from the Wharton School of Business. Wendy finds balance as a rowing and high-school theater fan, a universal design afficionado, an aspiring gardener and furniture-maker and walking (and talking) with others through forests, mountains and cities.

Endnotes

1. "Glennon Doyle and Brene on Untamed," *Unlocking Us with Brene Brown* Podcast, March 24, 2020. https://www.listennotes.com/podcasts/unlocking-us-with/glennon-doyle-and-bren%C3%A9-on-YGM0Il5B2Pn/#1

2. To understand how path breaking these nominations were, consider that women were not permitted to wear pantsuits (or pants of any kind) on the US Senate floor until 1993, when Senators Barbara Mikulski and Carol Moseley Braun wore pants onto the floor in defiance of the rule until the rule was amended later that year by Senate Sergeant-at-Arms Martha Pope.

3. There are a number of articles written examining whether the '90s were a setback for women such as "How they Tricked Women into Thinking They'd Gained Gender Equality," Time.com. Excerpted from Yarrow, Allison, *90s Bitch: Media Culture and the Failed Promise of Gender Equality*, Harper Perennial, June 2018.

4. Premack, Rachel and Ward, Marguerite, "What is a Microaggression? 14 things people think are fine to say at work are actually racist, sexist or offensive," *Business Insider*, March 21, 2021.

5. Hassan, Kamal; Varadan, Monisha; Zeisberger, Claudia. "How the VC Pitch Process is Failing Female Entrepreneurs," *Harvard Business Review*, January 2020.

6. Folkman, Joseph and Zenger, Jack; "Research: Women Score Higher Than Men in Most Leadership Tests," *Harvard Business Review*, June 2019.

7. Duhigg, Charles, "What Google Learned from its Quest to Build the Perfect Team," *New York Times*, February 2016.

8. Sandberg, Sheryl, *Lean In: Women, Work and the Will to Lead*, Alfred A. Knopf, 2013.

9. Slaughter, Anne-Marie, *Why Women Still Can't Have It All*, The Atlantic, July/August 2012. https://www.theatlantic. com/magazine/archive/2012/07/why-women-still-cant-have-it-all/309020/

10. Scott, Kim, *Radical Candor: Be a Kick-Ass Boss Without Losing Your Humanity*, St. Martin's Press, 2017.

11. Multiple books of inspiration by Brene Brown: *Gifts of Imperfection: Let Go of Who You Think You're Supposed to Be and Embrace Who You Are* (2010); *Daring Greatly: How the Courage to be Vulnerable Transforms the Way we Live, Love, Parent, and Lead* (2012); *Braving the Wilderness* (2017); and *Daring to Lead: Brave Work; Tough Conversations; Whole Hearts* (2018).

12. Colonna, Jerry. *Reboot* Podcast Episode #93, "Standing in the Gap with Amy Nelson," October 2018.

13. Christiansen, Clay, *The Innovator's Dilemma: When New Technologies Cause Great Firms to Fail*, Harper Business, 2016. Clayton Christensen first published his seminal research chronicling how new technologies cause great firms to fail, as they find it difficult to divert resources away from their historic sources of success.

14. Isaacson, Walter, *The Innovators: How a Group of Hackers, Geniuses and Geeks Created the Digital Revolution*, Simon & Schuster, 2015.

15. For the same reason, companies looking to increase the women in their ranks learn to pare down the list of "qualifications," as research shows women may self-select out of applying if they don't meet certain requirements. Mohr, Tara Sophia, "Why Women Don't Apply for Jobs Unless They're 100% Qualified," *Harvard Business Review*, August 2014.

16. Ann Mehl, Nonviolent Communication https://www. annmehl.com/nonviolent-communication/

17. Goldsmith, Marshall, *What Got You Here Won't Get You*

There: How Successful People Get Even More Successful, Random House, 2007.

18. PWC, "US Remote Work Study: It's Time to Reimagine Where and How Work Will Get Done," January 2021.

19. McKinsey & Company, LeanIn.org, "Women in the Workplace 2020," September 2020.

20. https://www.ecb.europa.eu/press/tvservices/podcast/html/ecb.pod210308_episode15.en.html "Fighting Biases and Empowering Women: A Conversation with Christian Lagarde and Ursula Von Der Leyen on Female Leadership and Gender Equality," *The ECB Podcast*, March 2021.

21. https://www.youtube.com/watch?v=Mh4f9AYRCZY. BBC News, "Children Interrupt BBC New Interview," March 2017.

22. The Way Women Work Blog: https://thewaywomenwork.com/2019/11/how-and-why-dads-of-daughters-are-leaders-in-womens-advancement/

23. Parental Leave in Iceland Gives Dad a Strong Position, *Nordic Labor Journal*, April 2019. http://www.nordiclabourjournal.org/i-fokus/in-focus-2019/future-of-work-iceland/article.2019-04-11.9299118347#:~:text=Iceland's%20new%20parental%20leave%20legislation,both%20to%20share%20between%20them

24. McKinsey & Company, LeanIn.org, "Women in the Workplace 2020," September 2020.

25. Roy, Eleanor Ainge "Jacinda Ardern makes history with baby Neve at UN general assembly," The Guardian, September 2018.

26. Rosling, Hans; Rosling, Ola; Ronn, Anna Rosling; *Factfulness: Ten Reasons Why We're Wrong about the World – And Why Things Are Better Than You Think*, Hodder & Stoughton, 2018.

27. For example, *Untangled: Guiding Teenage Girls Through the Seven Transitions into Adulthood* by Lisa Damour helped

contextualize and manage the insecurities and physical changes our daughters confront as they graduate from adolescence.

28. Hallowell, Edward, *The Childhood Roots of Adult Happiness: Five Steps to Help Kids Create and Sustain Lifelong Joy.* Ballantine Books, NY 2002.

29. Duckworth, Angela, *Grit: The Power of Passion and Perseverance*, Simon & Schuster, 2016.

30. Damour, Lisa PhD. *Untangled: Guiding Teenage Girls Through the Seven Transitions Into Adulthood*, Ballantine Books, 2016.

31. "Warren Buffett says the most important decision you'll ever make has nothing to do with your money or career," CNBC, May 2018.

32. McKinsey & Company, LeanIn.org, "Women in the Workplace 2020," September 2020.

33. LeanIn.org and SurveyMonkey, *Women are Maxing Out and Burning Out During COVID-19*, May 7, 2020, https://leanin.org/article/womens-workload-and-burnout

34. Grose, Jessica, "Why Women Do the Household Worrying, and how to get men to do more of it," New York Times Parenting Newsletter April 22, 2021, https://www.nytimes.com/2021/04/21/parenting/women-gender-gap-domestic-work.html

35. https://www.theatlantic.com/magazine/archive/2015/10/why-i-put-my-wifes-career-first/403240/

36. Esther Perel, acclaimed couples' therapist, was hired by Silicon Valley venture firm, First Round, to coach start up founders: https://firstround.com/review/how-to-fix-the-co-founder-fights-oure-sick-of-having-lessons-from-couples-therapist-esther-perel/

37. Anne Marie Slaughter calls us to "redefine the arc of a successful career" to be more realistic about these pulls from home. https://www.theatlantic.com/magazine/archive/2012/07/why-women-still-cant-have-it-all/309020/

38. Gottman, John M. PhD, Silver, Nan, *The Seven Principles for Making Marriages Work: A Practical Guide from the Country's Foremost Expert*, Three Rivers, 1999.

39. https://www.brucefeiler.com/wp-content/uploads/2019/10/Happy-Families-Toolkit-1.pdf

40. Gerdeman, Dina, "Kids of Working Moms Grow into Happy Adults," HBS Working Knowledge, July 2018. https://hbswk.hbs.edu/item/kids-of-working-moms-grow-into-happy-adults

41. Bruce Feiler, *Life Is in the Transitions: Mastering Change at Any Age*, July 2020.

42. Harding, Keith; Queen, Douglass, "Societal Pandemic Burnout: A COVID Legacy," Wiley Public Health Emergency Collection, July 2020. https://www.ncbi.nlm.nih.gov/pmc/articles/PMC7362153/

43. Collins, Jim; Porras, Jerry, *Built to Last: Successful Habits of Visionary Companies*, Harper Business, 1994.

44. SharpBrains is an independent market research firm tracking applied neuroscience.

45. Fernandez, Álvaro; Goldberg, Elkhonon; Michelon, Pascale. *The Sharpbrains Guide to Brain Fitness: How to Optimize Brain Health and Performance at Any Age*, 2013.

46. Vanderbilt, Tom, "You're Never Too Old to Become a Beginner," WSJ, January 2, 2021.

47. Huffington, Ariana. *Thrive: The Third Metric to Redefining Success and Creating a Life of Well-Being, Wisdom and Wonder.* Penguin Random House, 2014.

48. pepparent.org/wp-content/uploads/2018/06/Time-Management-Strategies-for-Busy-Parents-.pdf Paige Trevor.

49. Brookes, Arthur, *How to Build a Life,* https://www.theatlantic.com/projects/how-build-life/, column Atlantic Monthly.

50. Brookes, Arthur C. "The Three Equations for a Happy Life, Even During a Pandemic," *Atlantic Monthly,* April 9, 2020.

51. Sheryl Sandberg interview with Tiffany Dufu, Chief

Leadership Officer at Dufu. "Stop Trying to Do It All: Why Dropping the Ball Can Lead to Real Success" February 2017.

52. Ibid – Tiffany Dufu, "Stop Trying to Do it All."

53. Jerry Colonna talks about how to deal with this inner critic – the "Crow" on his shoulder – in his book *Reboot: Leadership and the Art of Growing Up.*

54. These "guideposts for wholehearted living and leading" were chronicled in Brene Brown's, *Daring Greatly: How the Courage to Be Vulnerable Transforms the Way We Live, Love, Parent, and Lead,* 2013.

55. Kondo, Marie, *The Life-Changing Joy of Tidying Up*, Clarkson Potter/Ten Speed, 2010.

56. McKeown, Greg, *Essentialism: The Disciplined Pursuit of Less,* Virgin Books, 2014.

57. "What to do When the World Is on Fire," by Maddy Pontz, *Ms Magazine,* October 2020.

58. FedEx Stolen Idea Commercial, https://www.youtube.com/watch?v=zNCrMEOqHpc

59. A helpful framework for non-violent communications, as originally put forth in by Marshal's seminal book, https://www.annmehl.com/nonviolent-communication/.

60. Parental Encouragement Program, https://pepparent.org/

61. Decade of trade liberalization (accelerating the flow of people across borders) and changing expectations of corporate commitments (moving towards more cost-effective labor contracts/"gig" workers) means commitments to companies are more tenuous.

62. A good resource on non-violent communications (observation, feelings, needs/values, requests) for kids is https://www.nonviolentcommunication.com/resources/articles-about-nvc/teen-communication/

63. One of the common practices is creating affinity groups so that under-represented employees can find kinship and

brainstorm solutions.

64. Johnson, Bea, TED Talk, https://www.youtube.com/watch?v=CSUmo-40pqA

65. Miller, Stephanie, *Zero-Waste Living the 80/20 Way*, Changemakers Books 2020

66. In 2015, Anne Marie Slaughter turned her 3 million plus viewed Atlantic article into a book *Unfinished Business: Women, Men, Work and Family.*

CHANGEMAKERS
BOOKS

Transform your life, transform *our* world. Changemakers
Books publishes books for people who seek to become positive,
powerful agents of change. These books inform, inspire, and
provide practical wisdom and skills to empower us to write
the next chapter of humanity's future.
www.changemakers-books.com

Resetting Our Future: Zero Waste Living, The 80/20 Way
The Busy Person's Guide to a Lighter Footprint
Stephanie J. Miller
Empowering the busy individual to do the easy things that
have a real impact on the climate and waste crises.

**Resetting Our Future: SMART Futures
for a Flourishing World**
A Paradigm Shift for Achieving Global Sustainability
Claire A. Nelson
SMART futures is a 'systems literacy' approach to problem
solving that allows us to address challenges of our volatile,
uncertain, complex and ambiguous world as an integrated
whole

**Resetting Our Future: Impact ED
How Community College Entrepreneurship Creates
Equity and Prosperity**
Andrew Gold, Mary Beth Kerly & Rebecca A. Corbin
This book provides leaders with a roadmap to the future,
showing how entrepreneurial thinking and action can put
local communities on the path to recovery from the economic
devastation induced by the COVID-19 pandemic.